Aphrodite

Lost

Time

Beach

Aphrodite

Lost

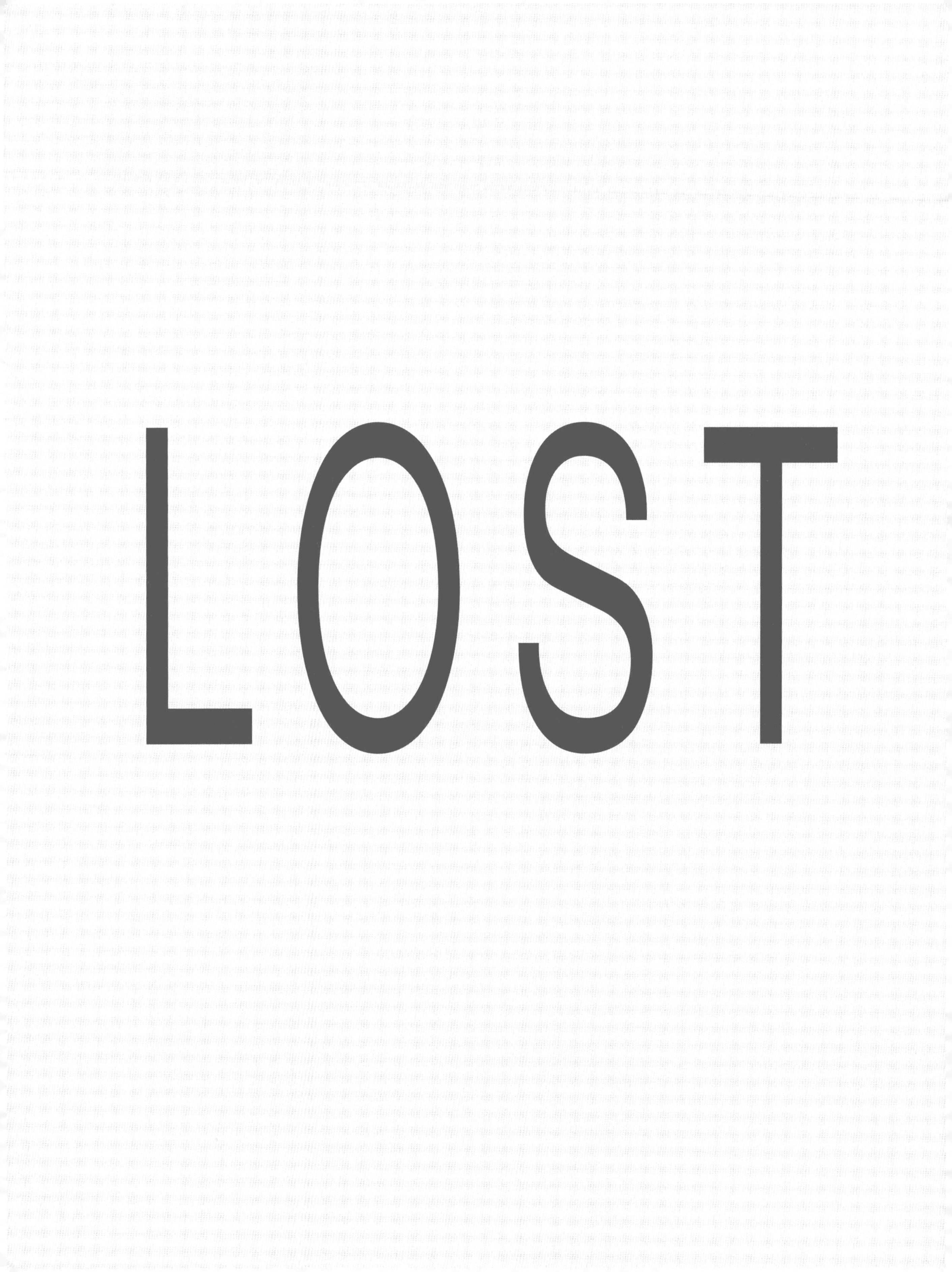
LOST

Lost

Time

Beach

Lost Time
Aphrodite Beach

Lost

Time

Beach

Louise Enhörning

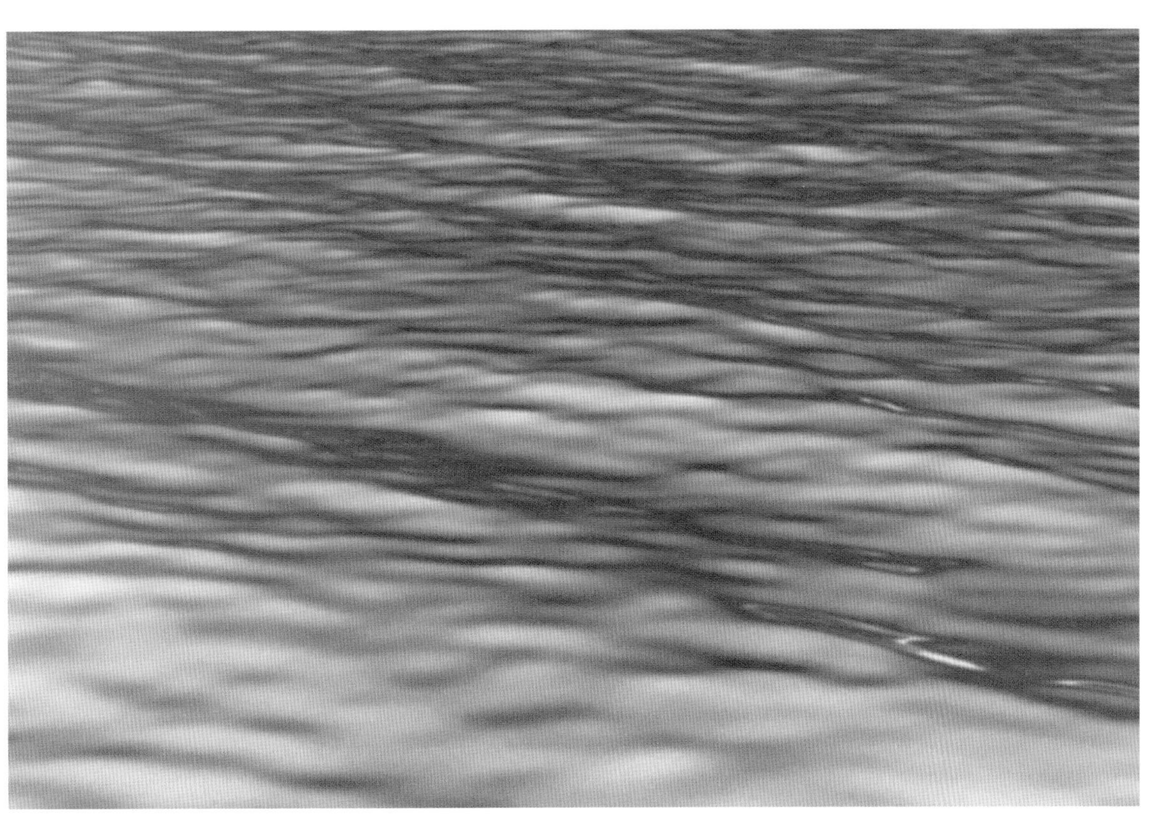

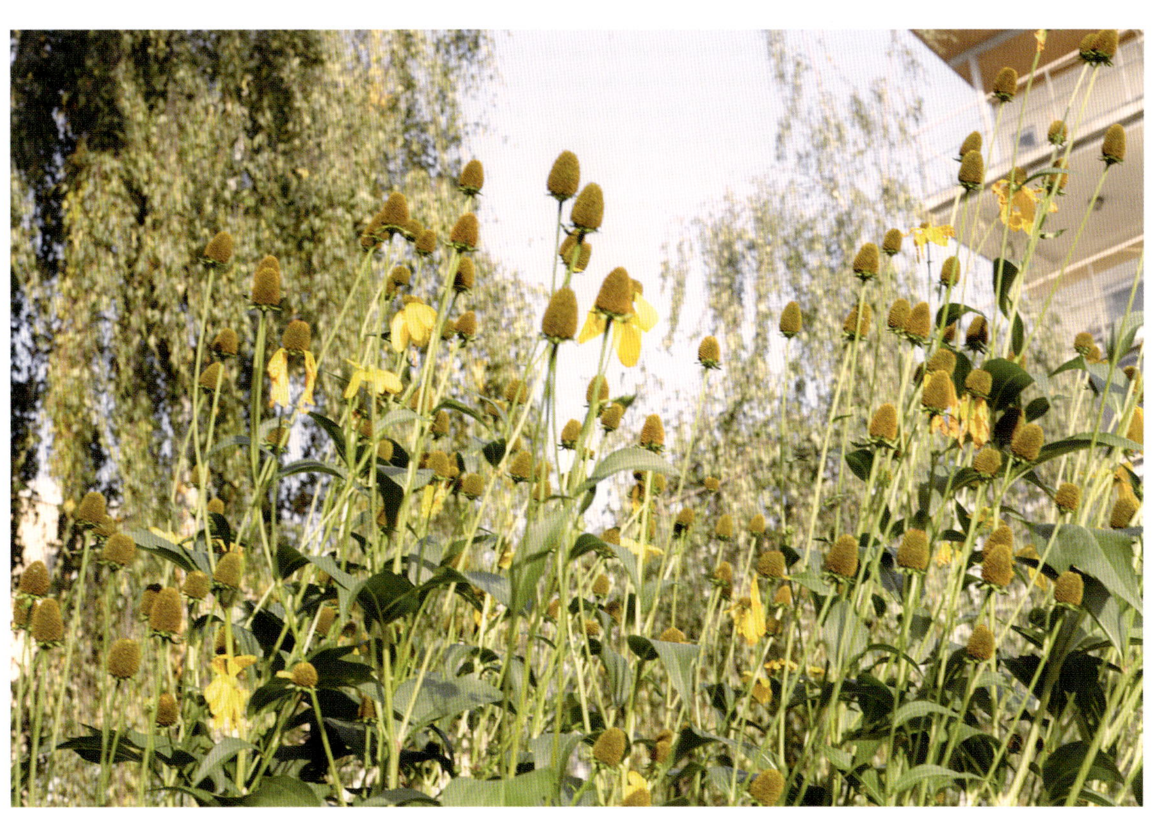

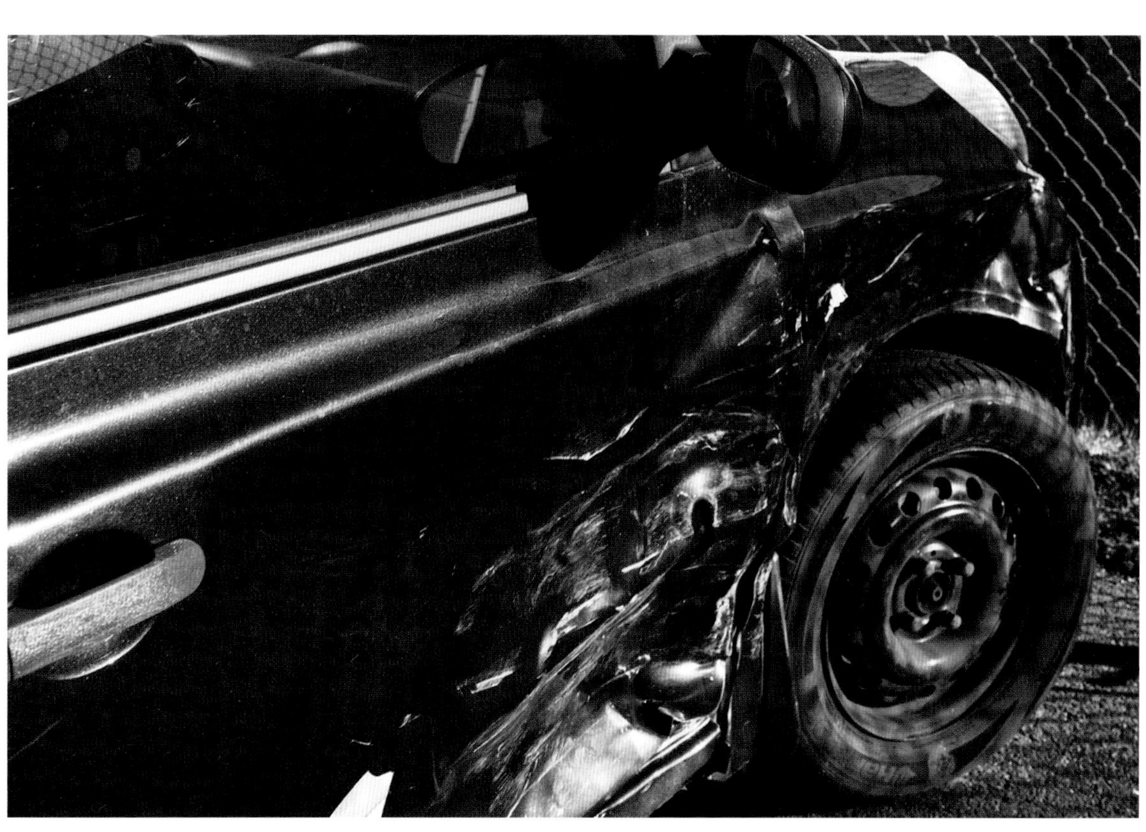

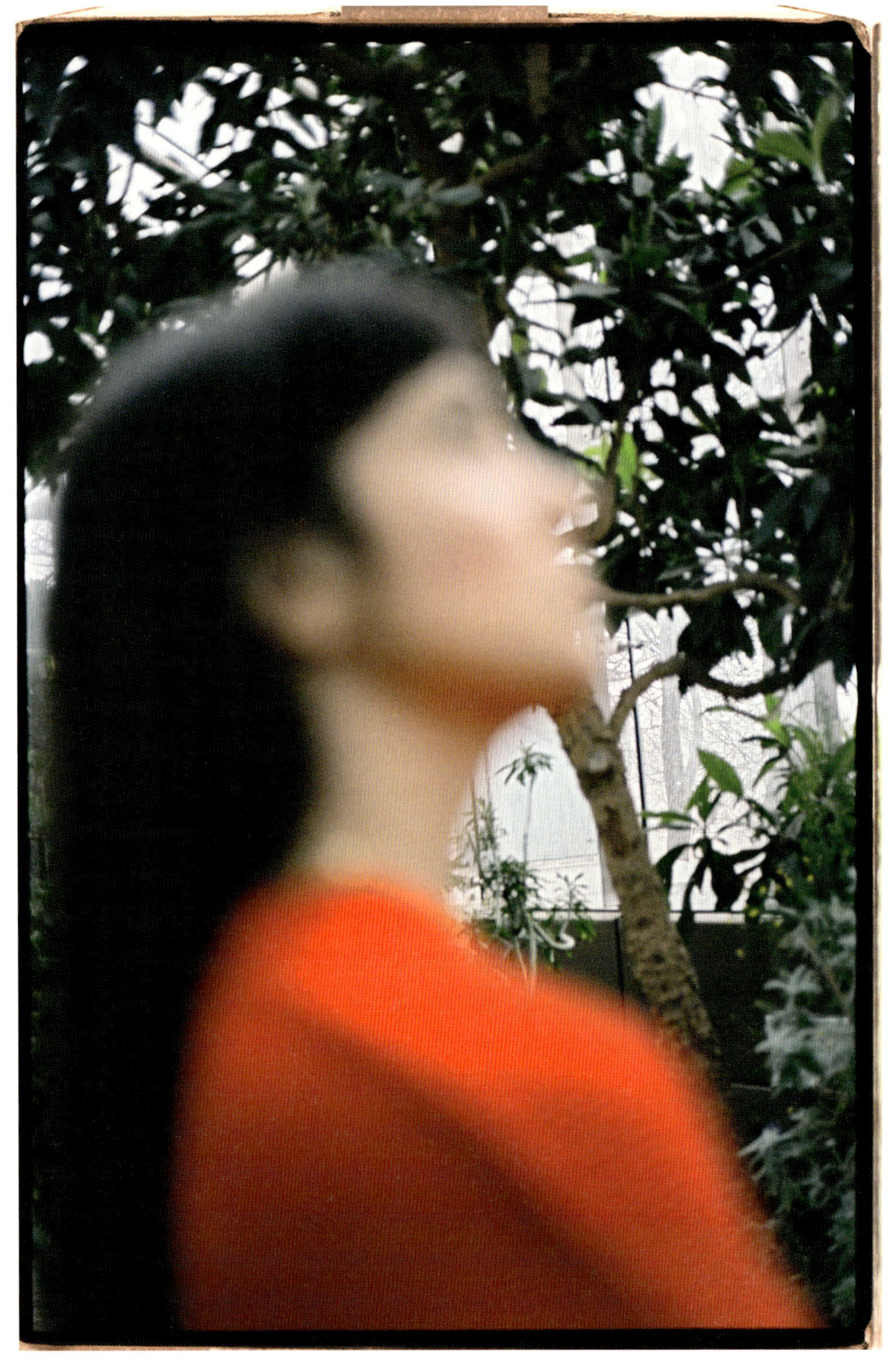

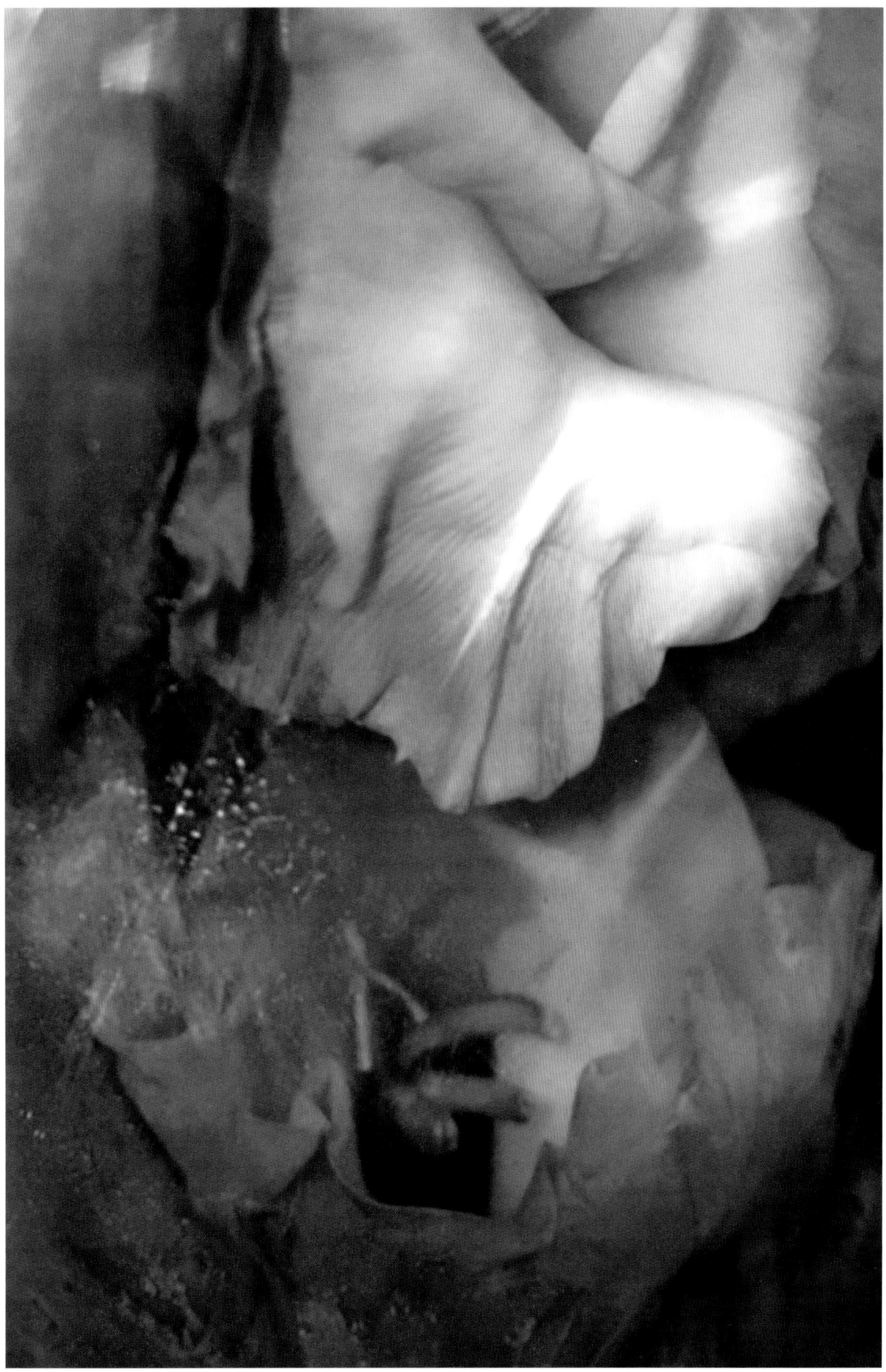

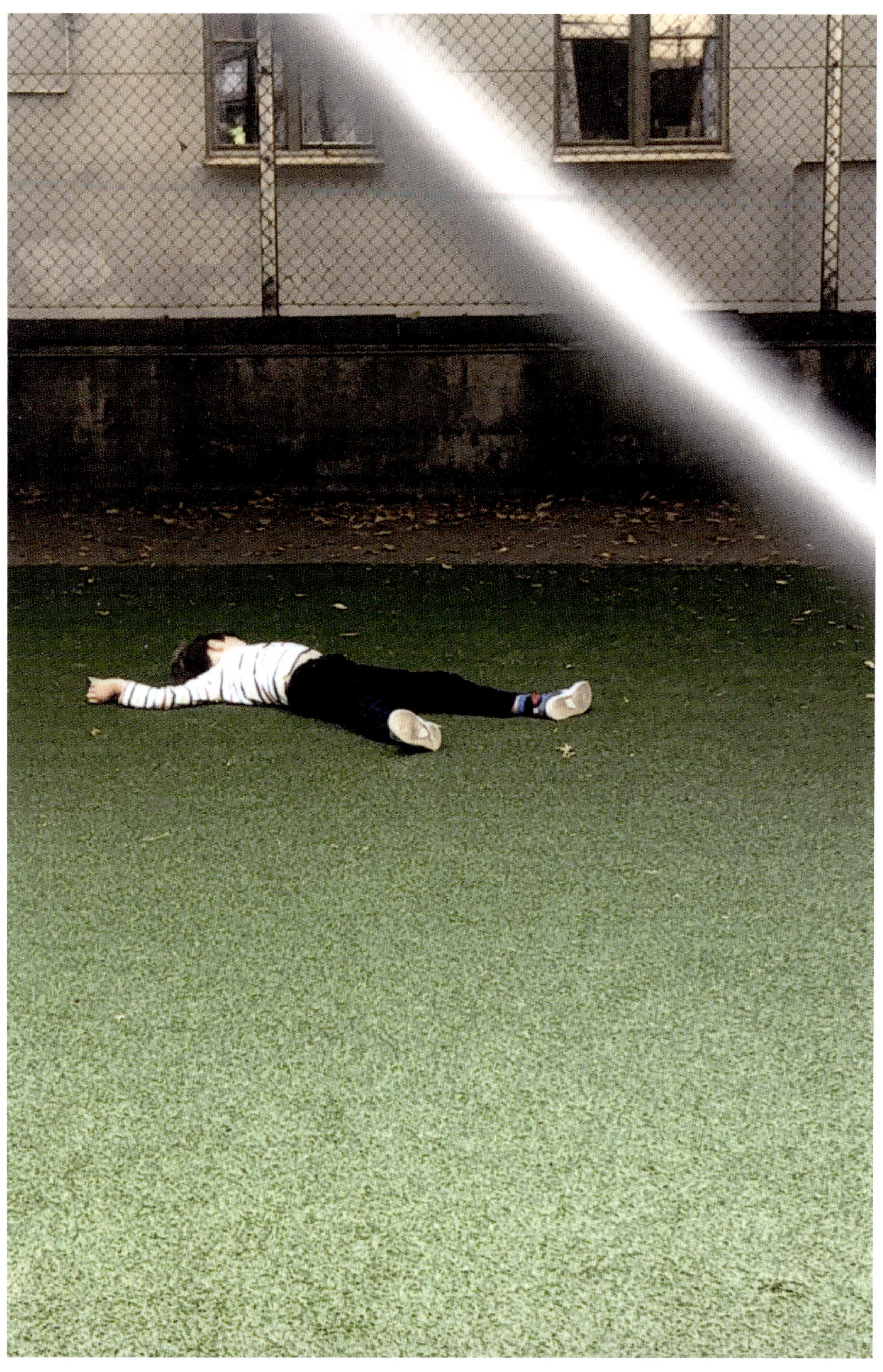

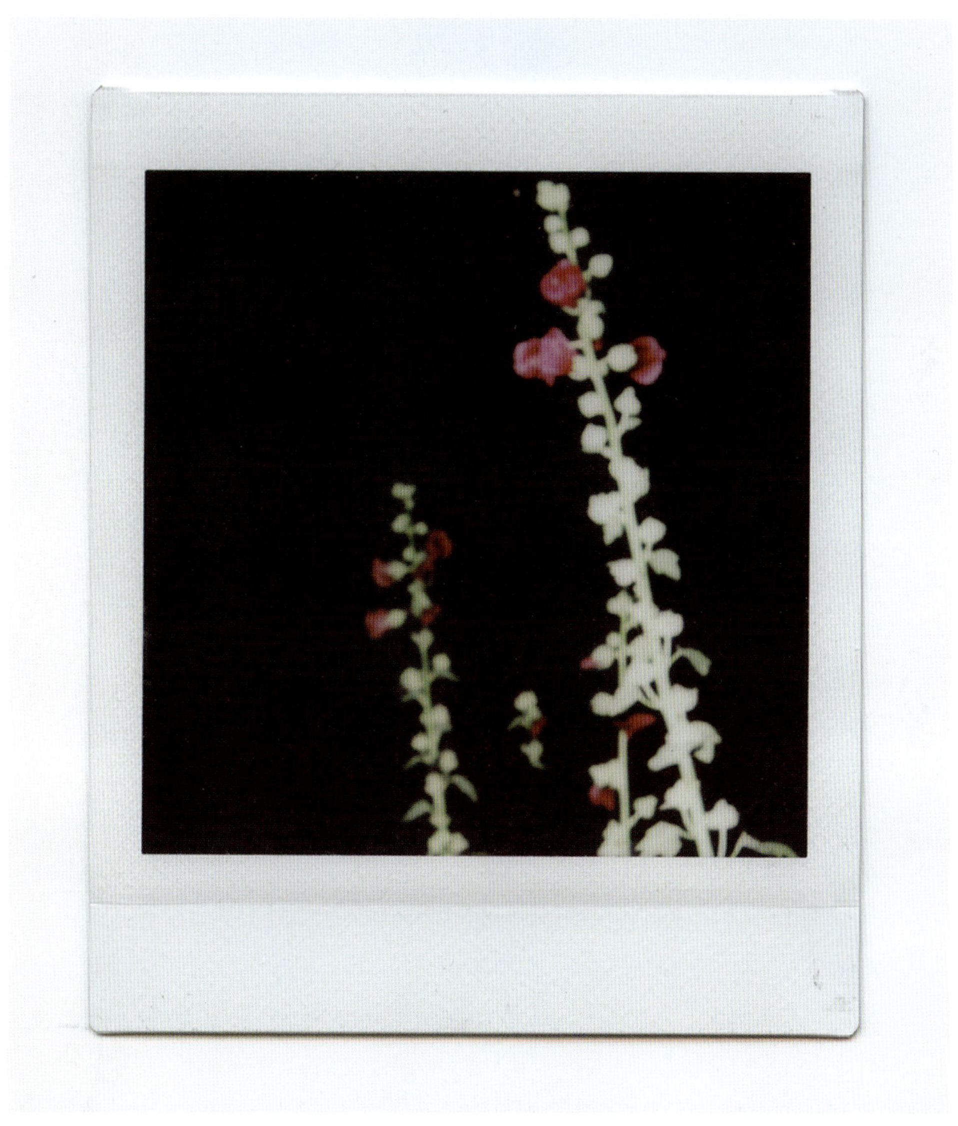

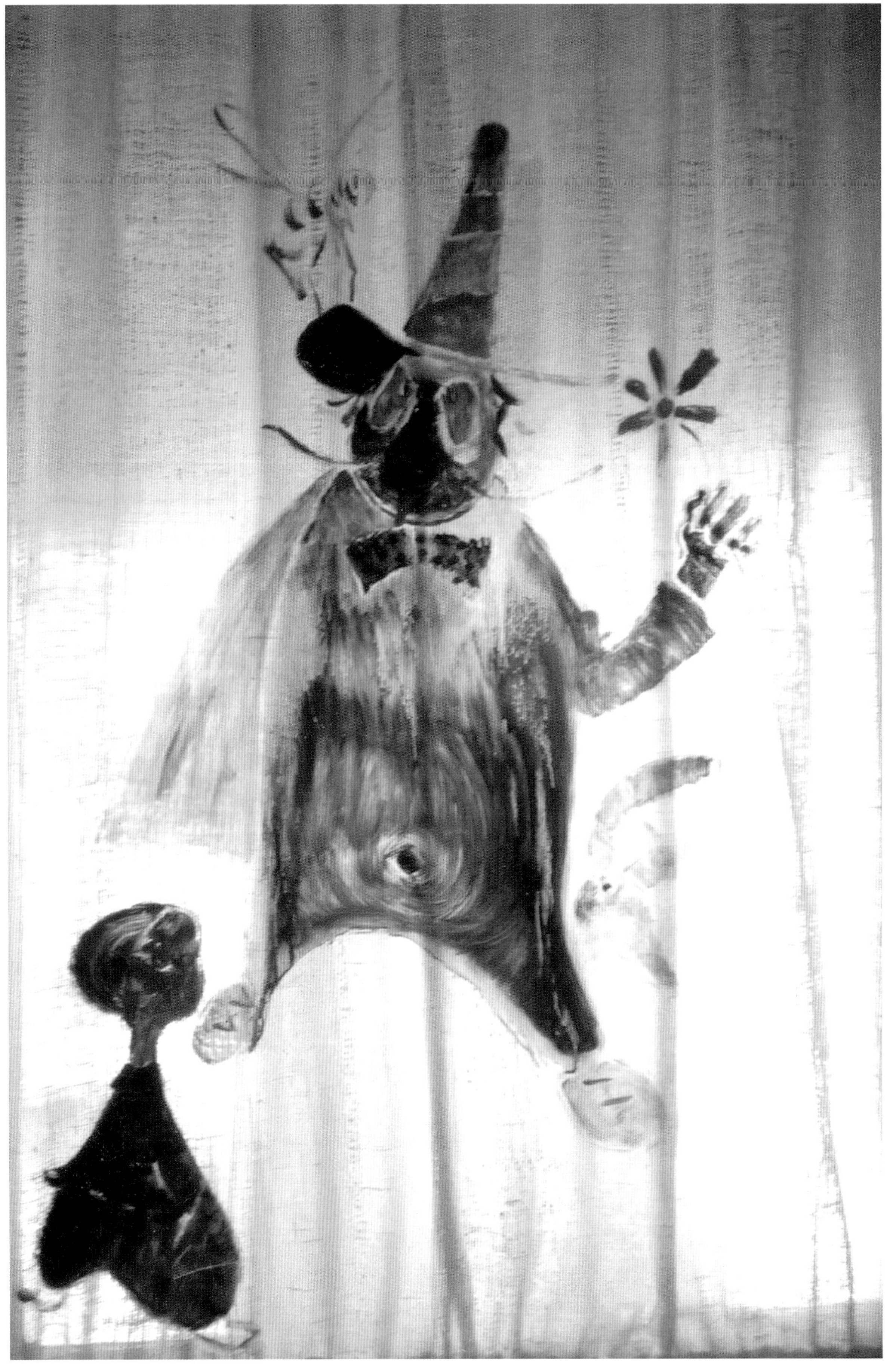

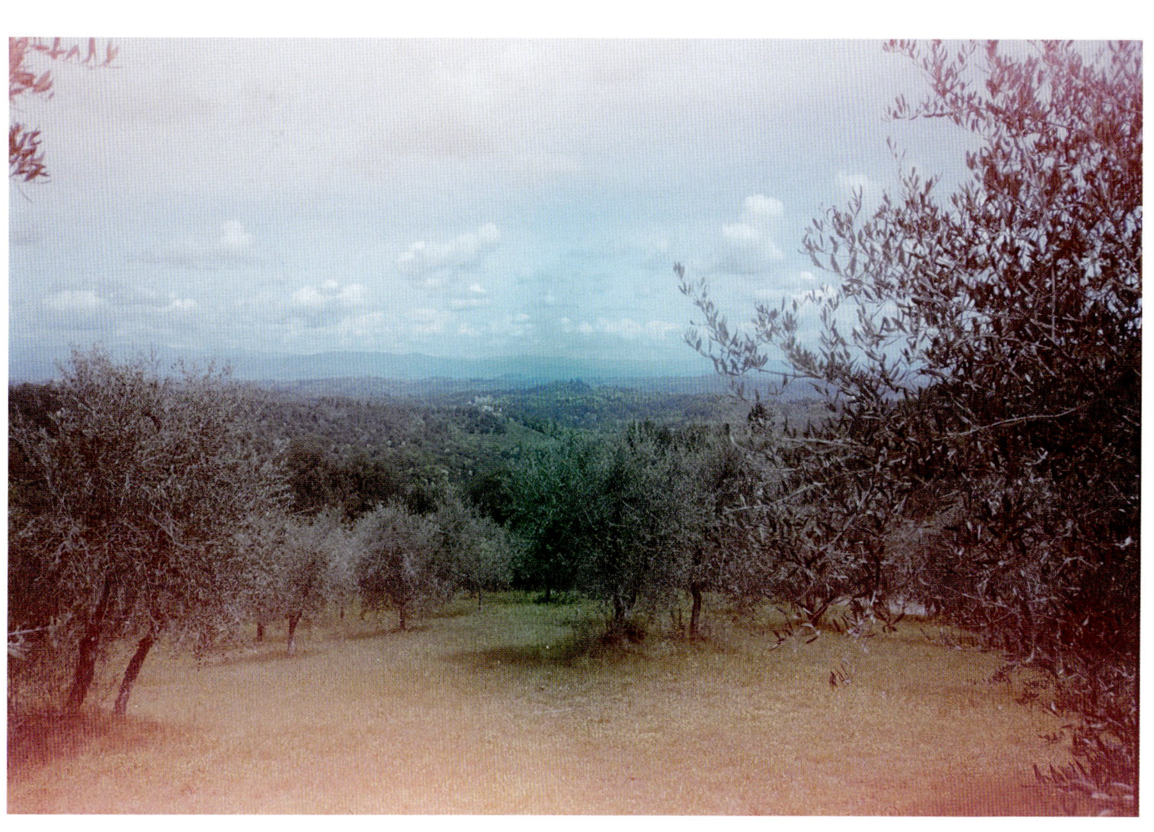

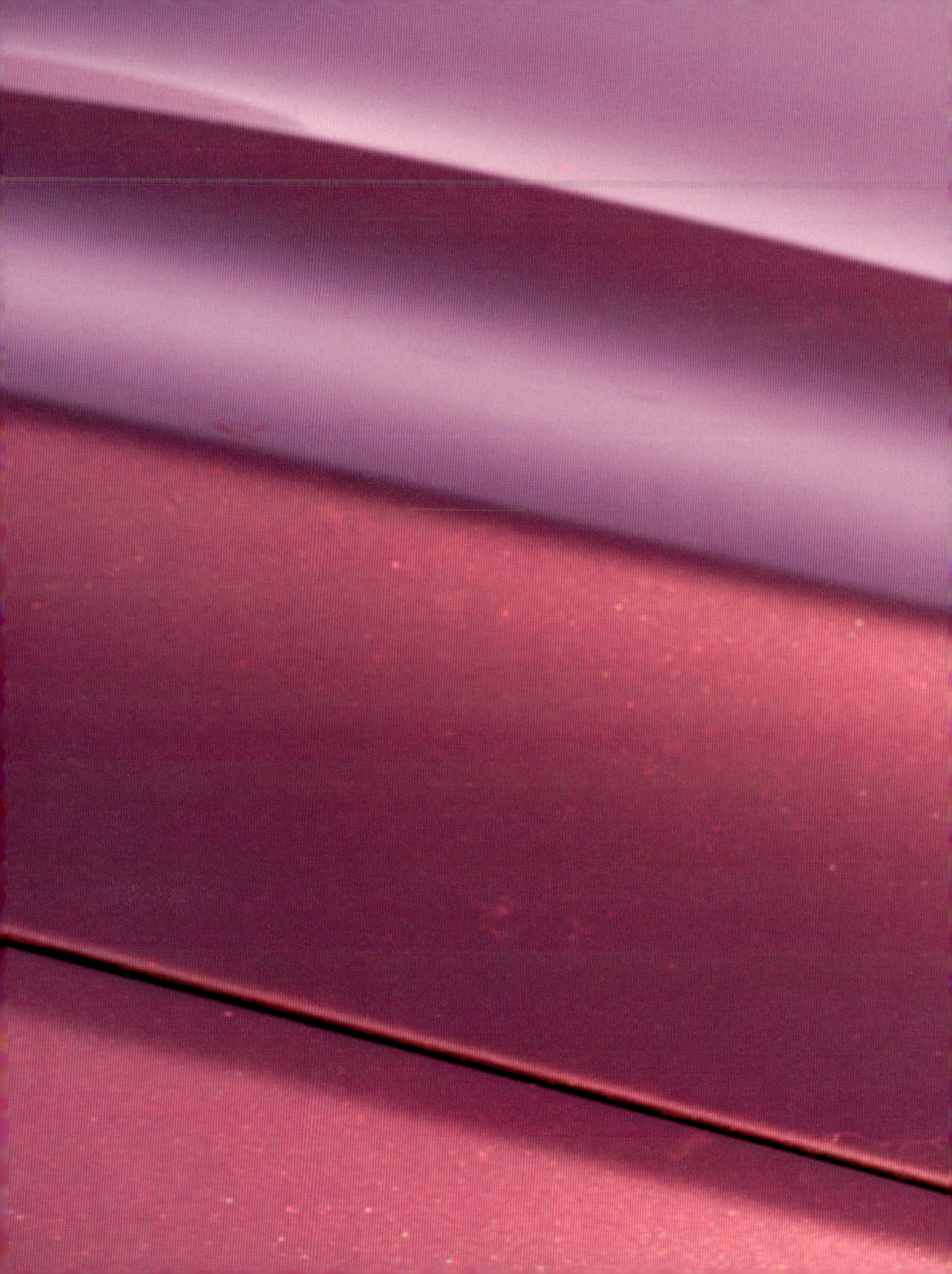

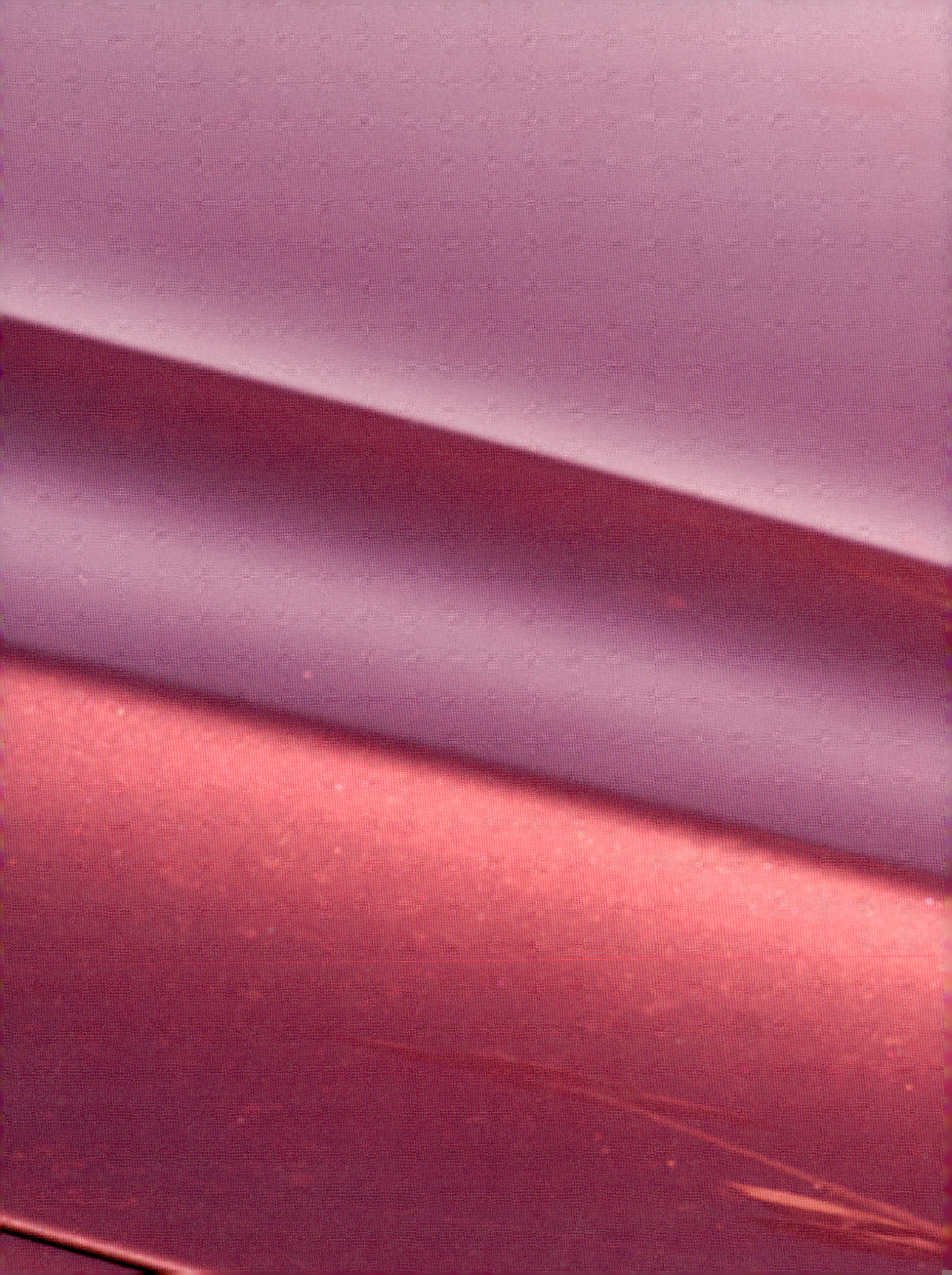

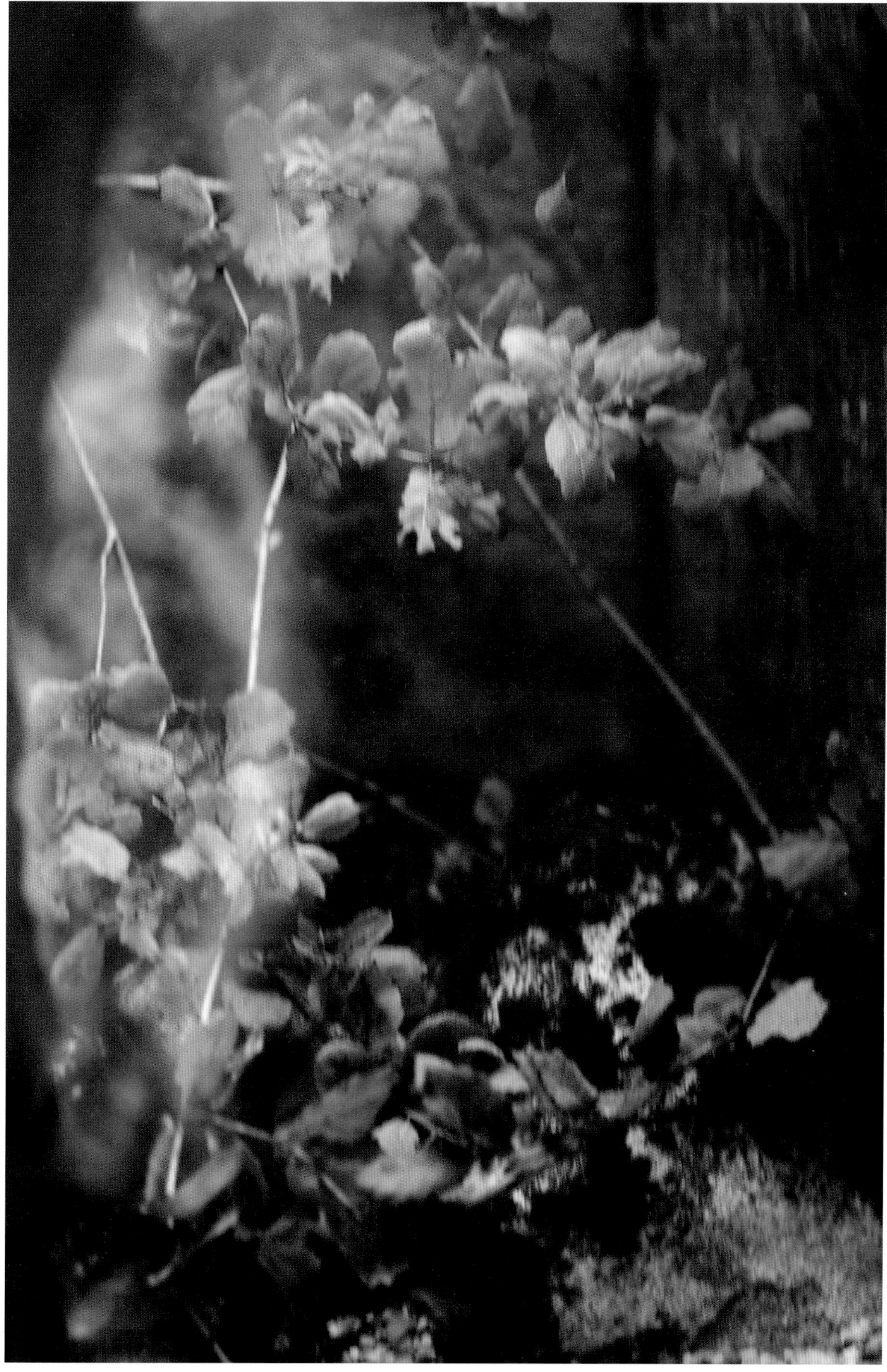

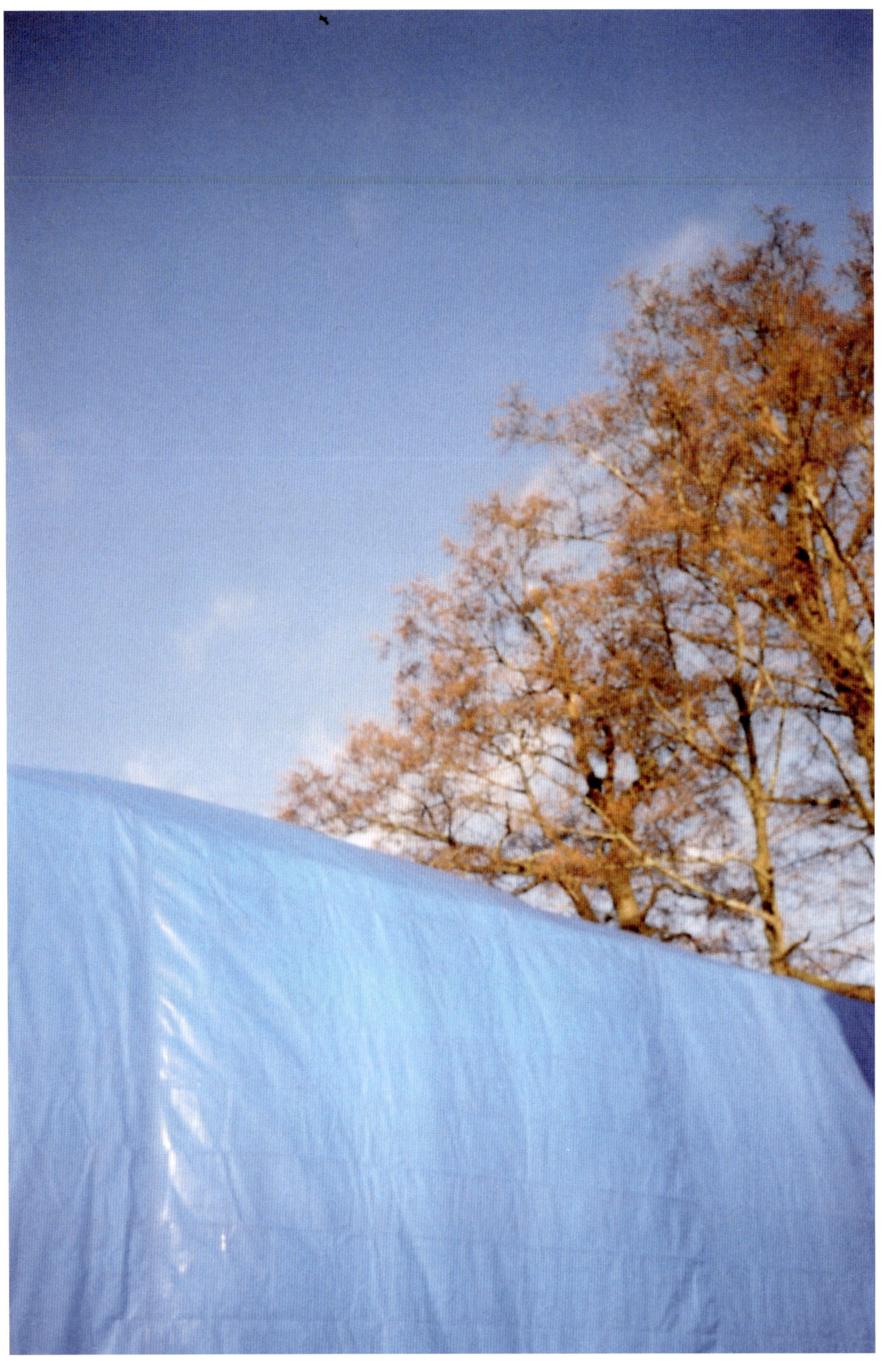

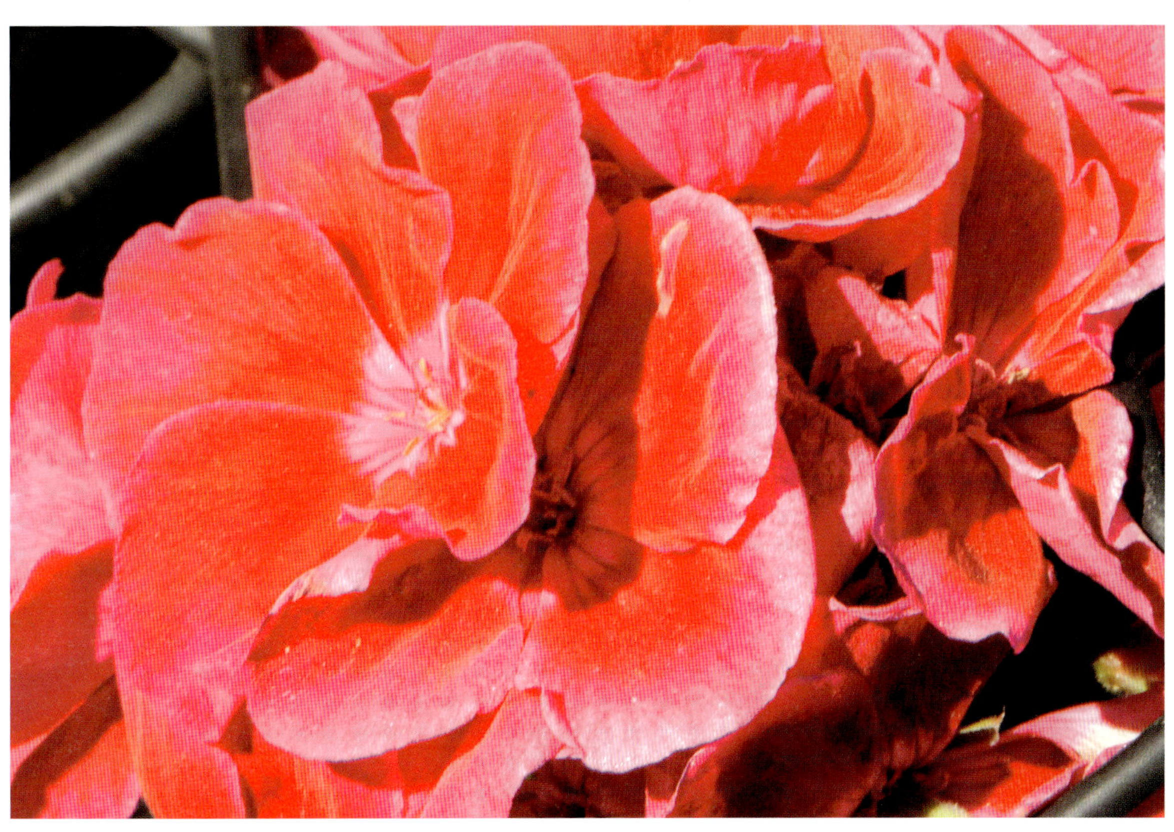

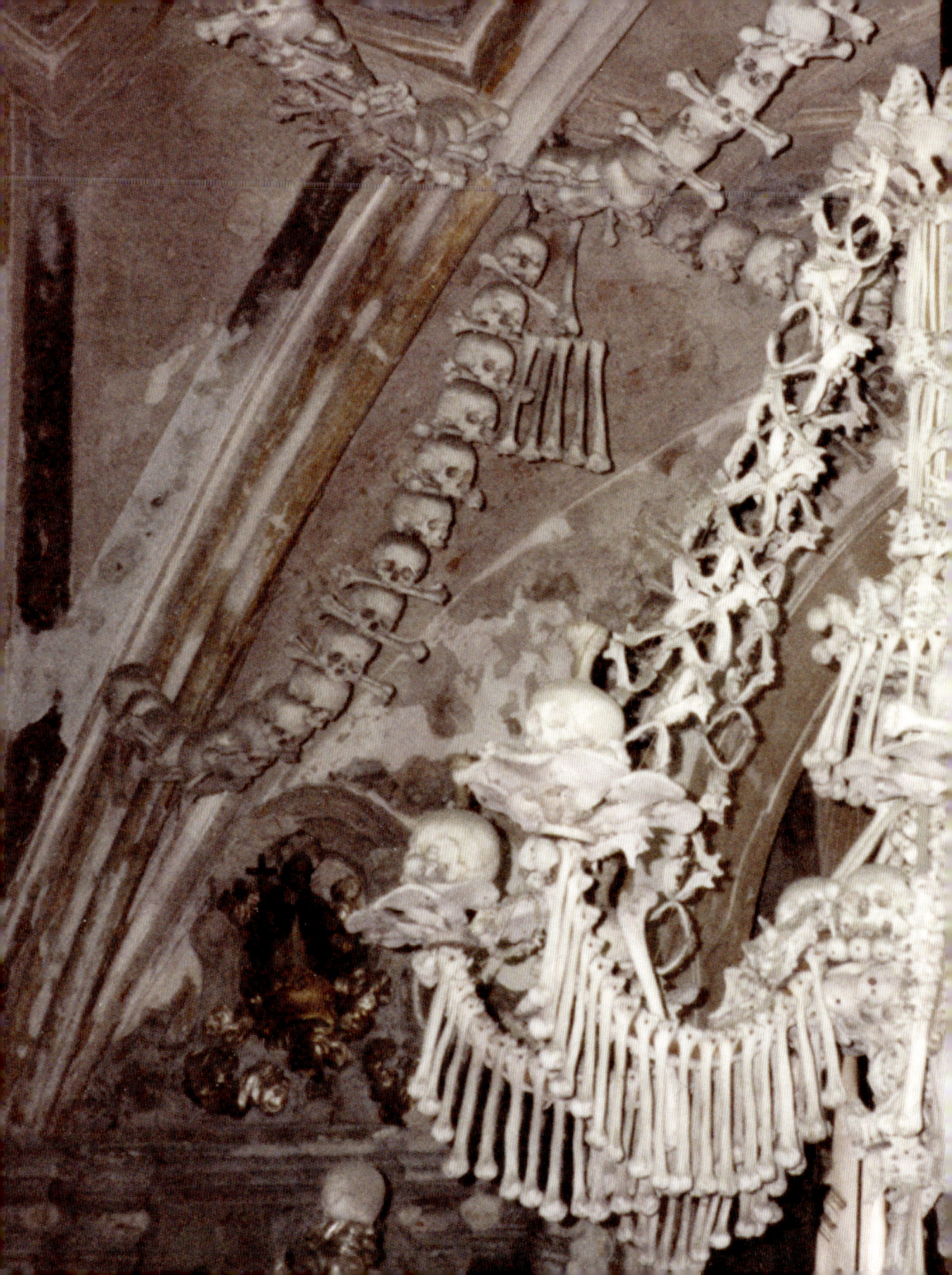

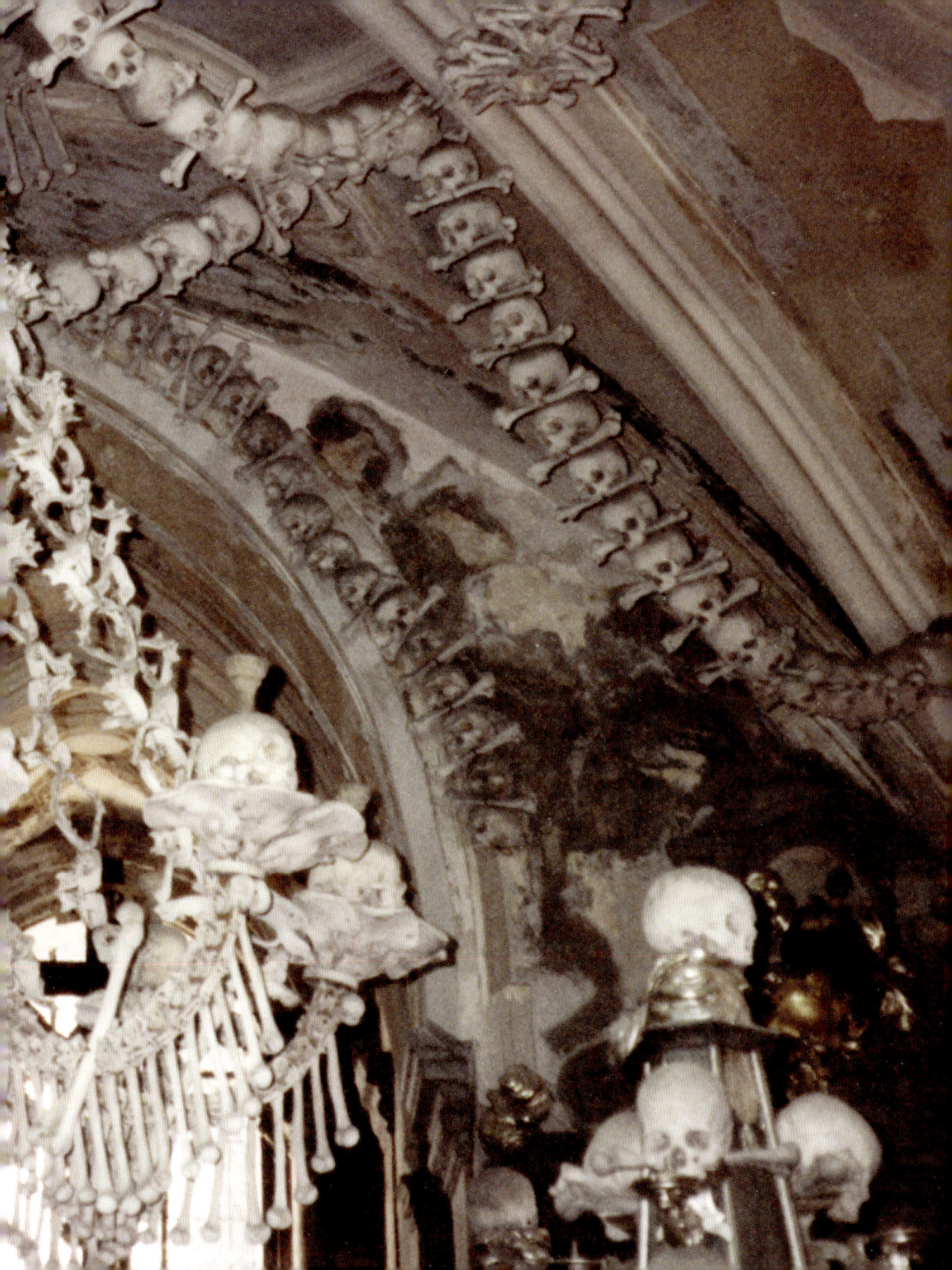

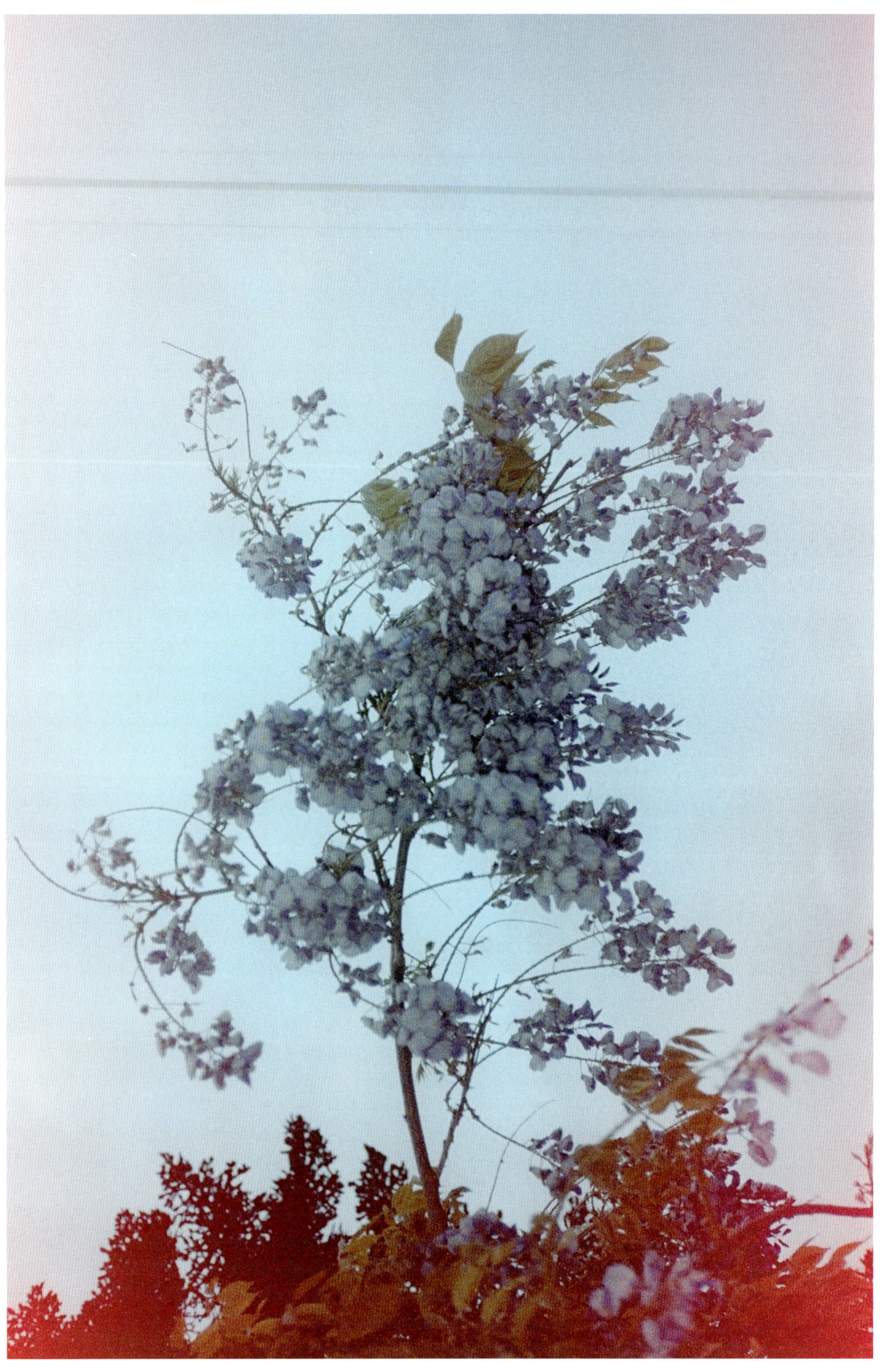

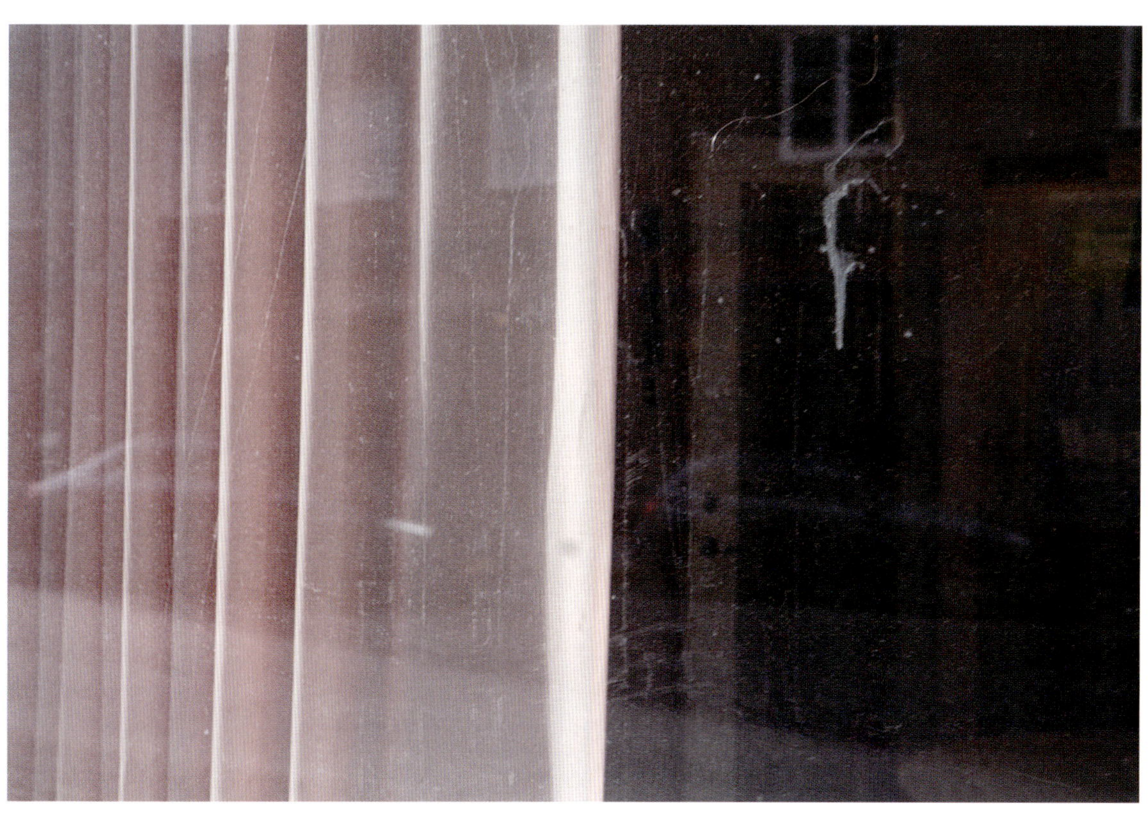

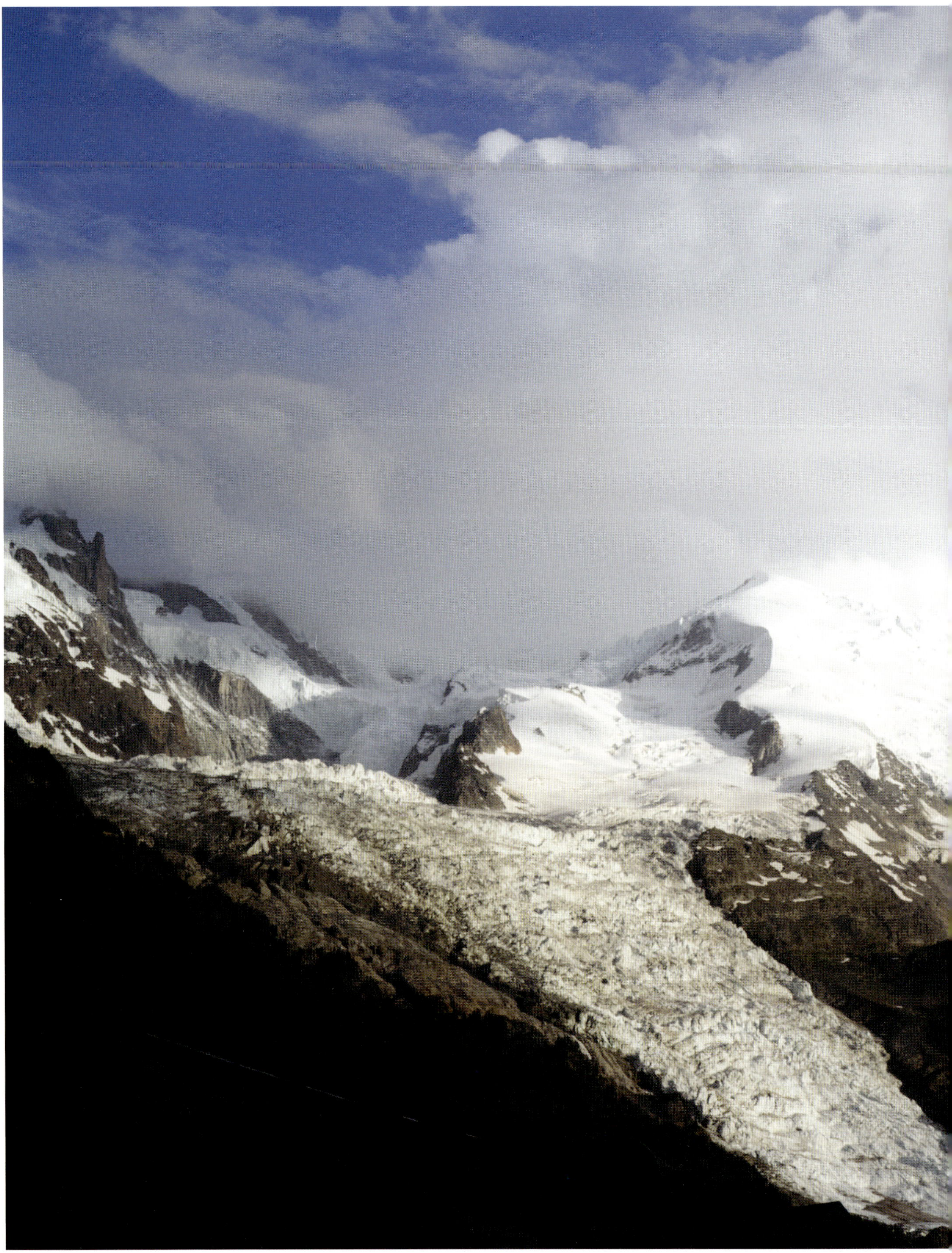

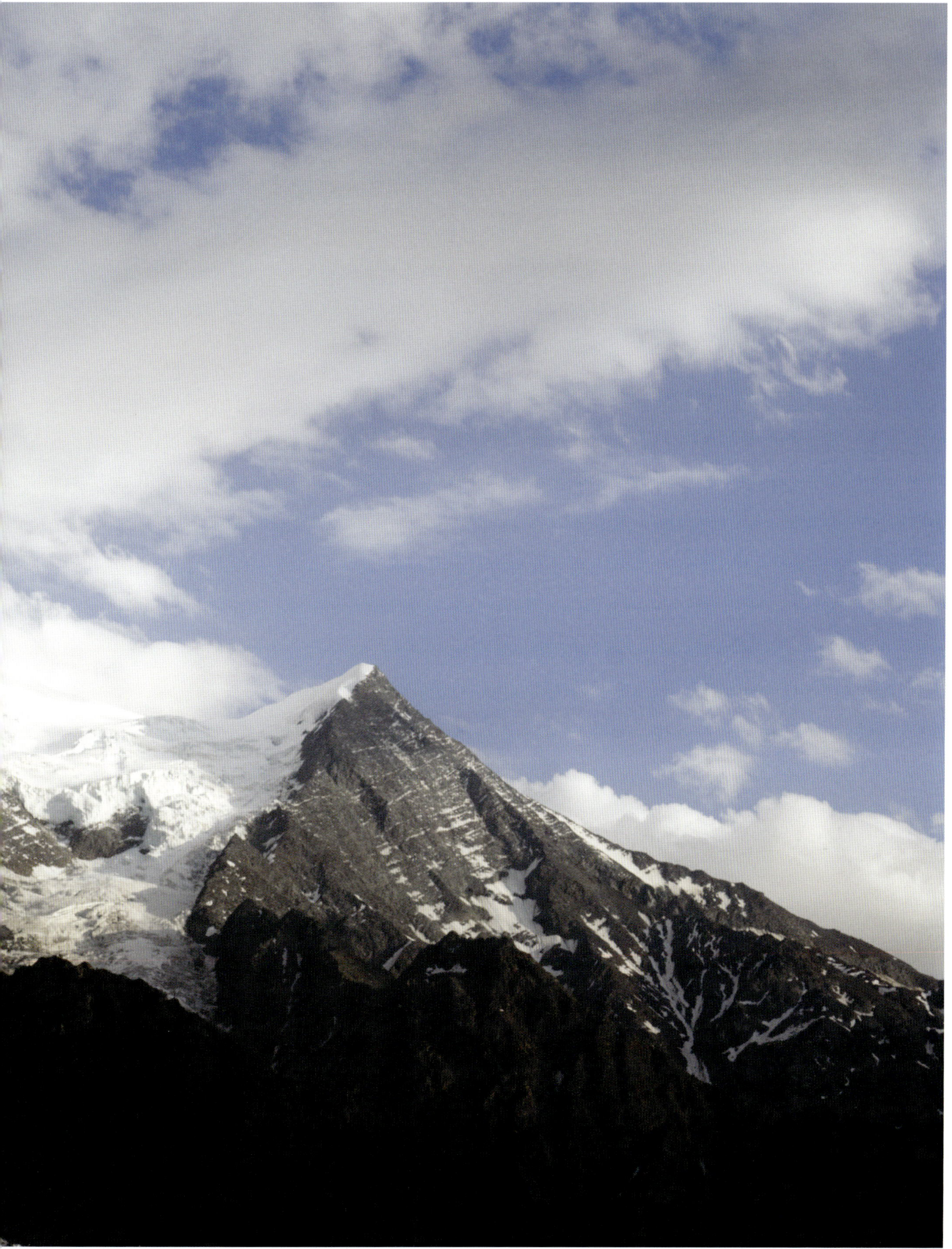

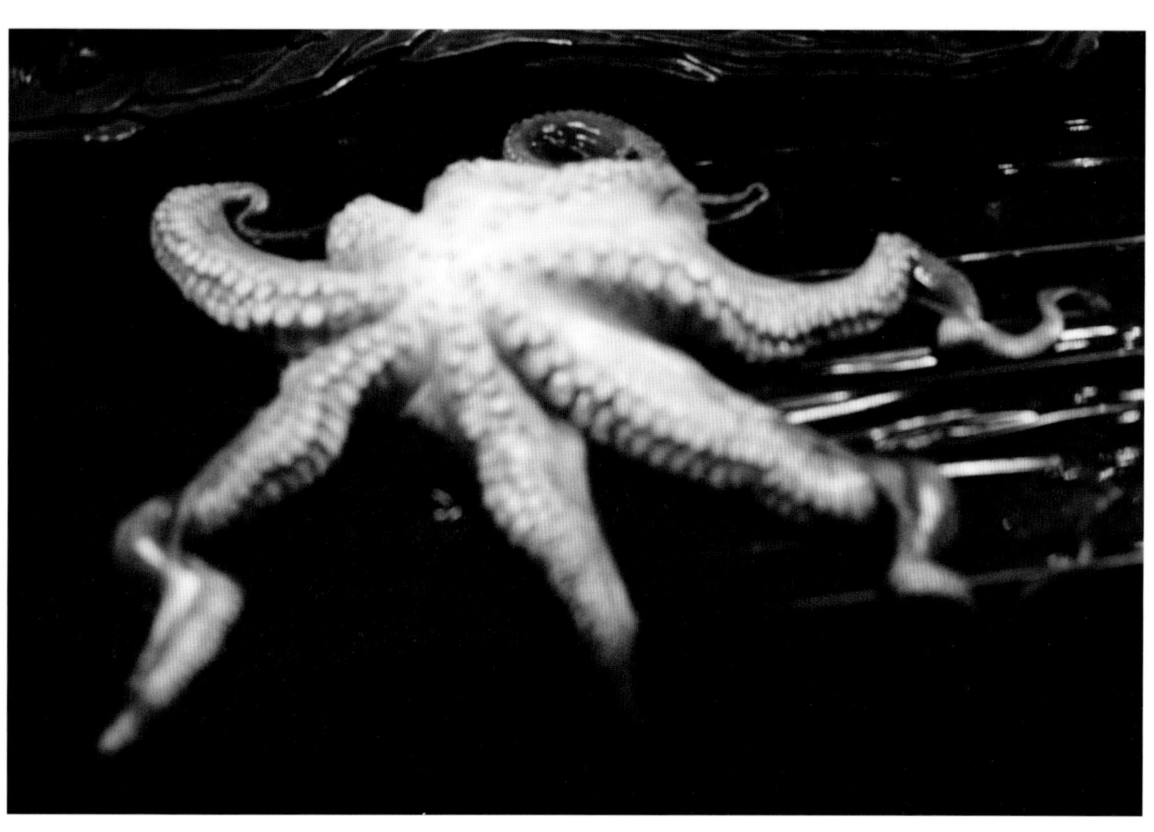

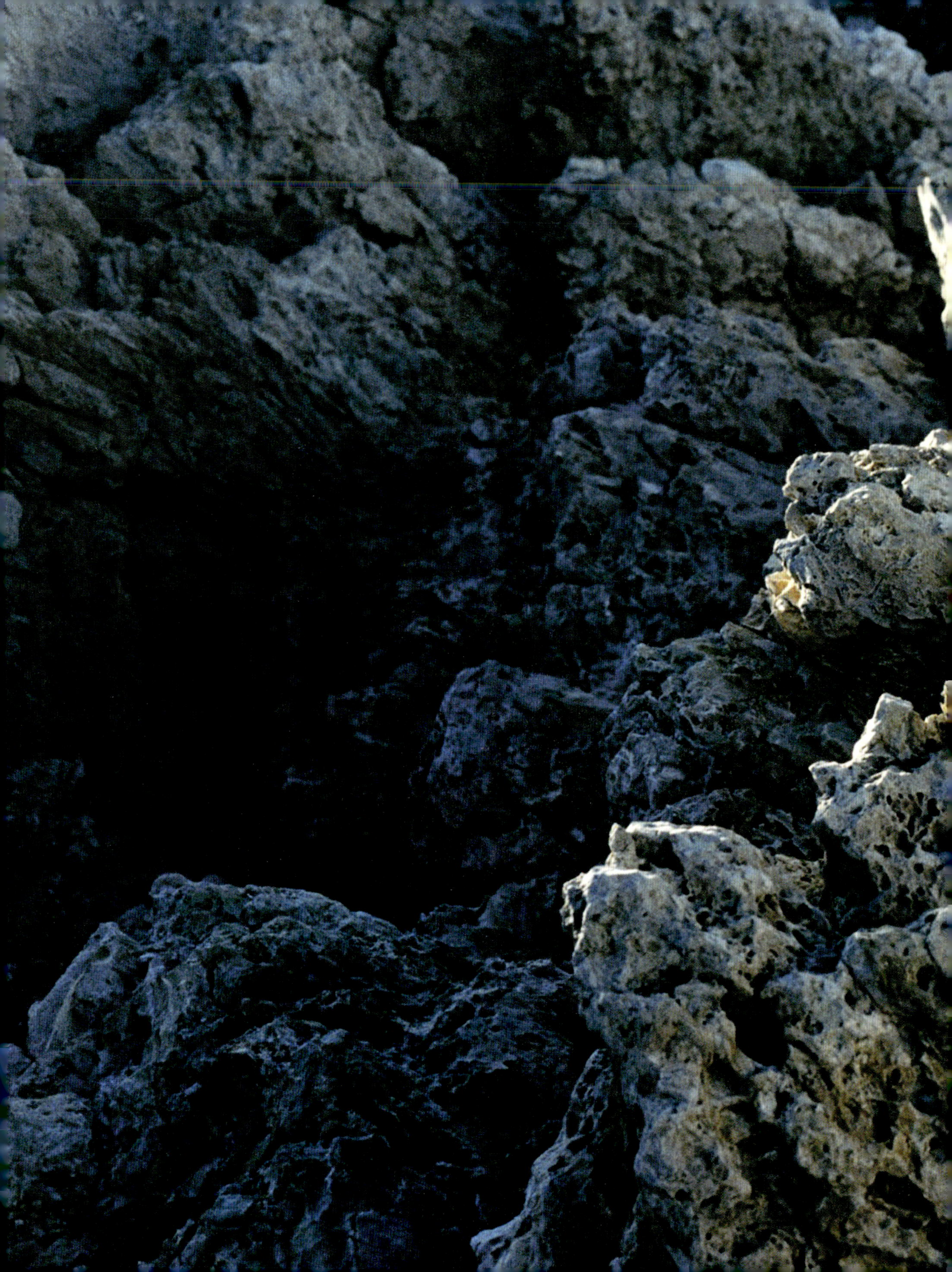

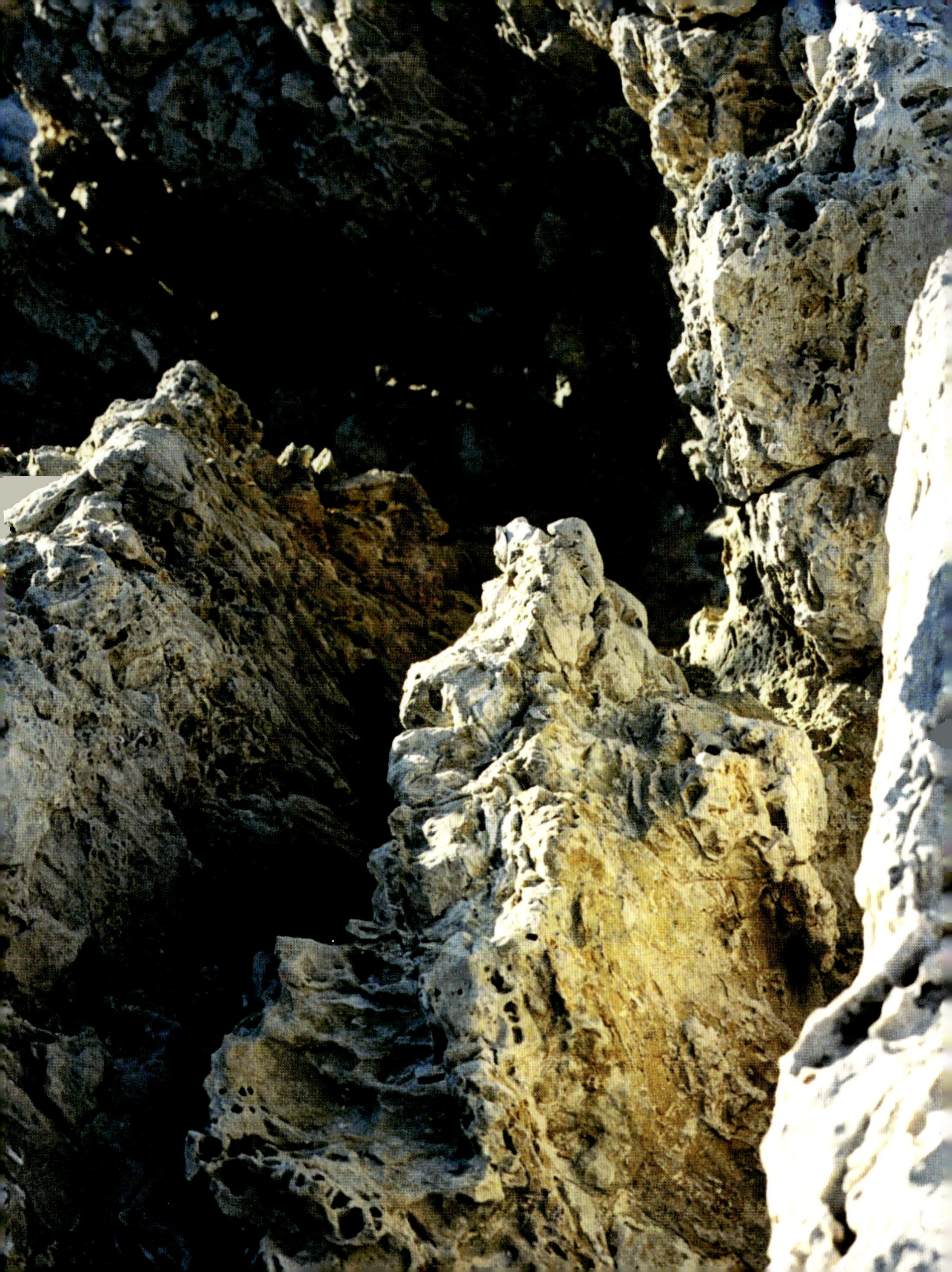

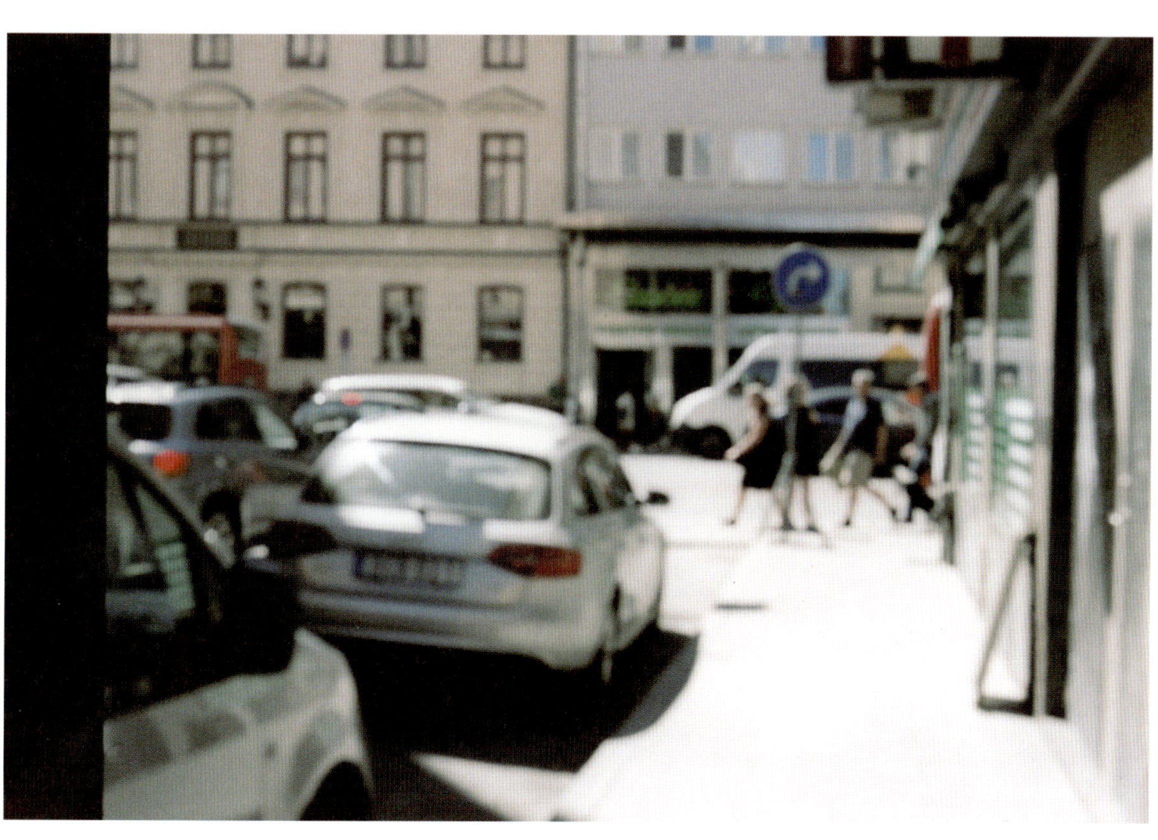

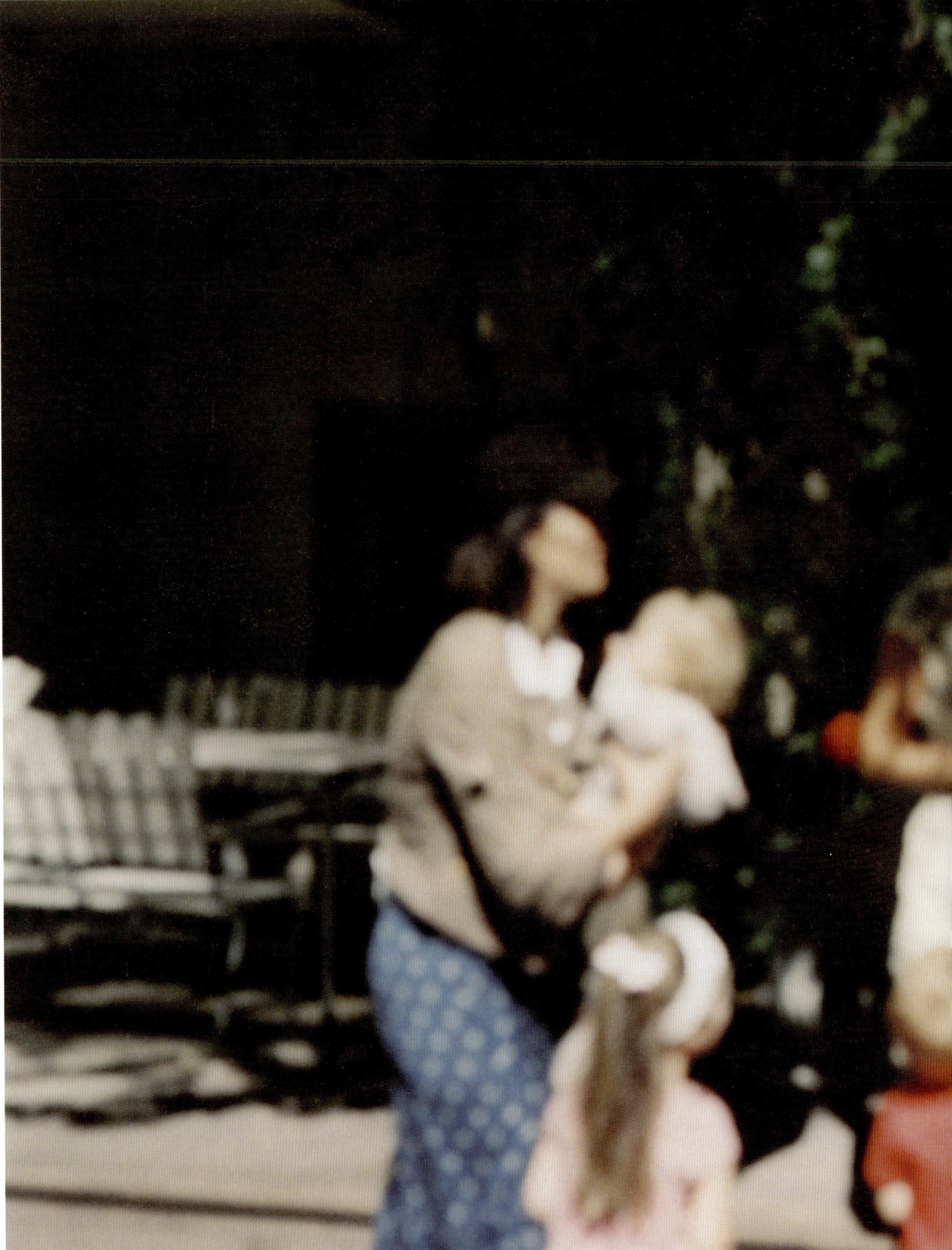

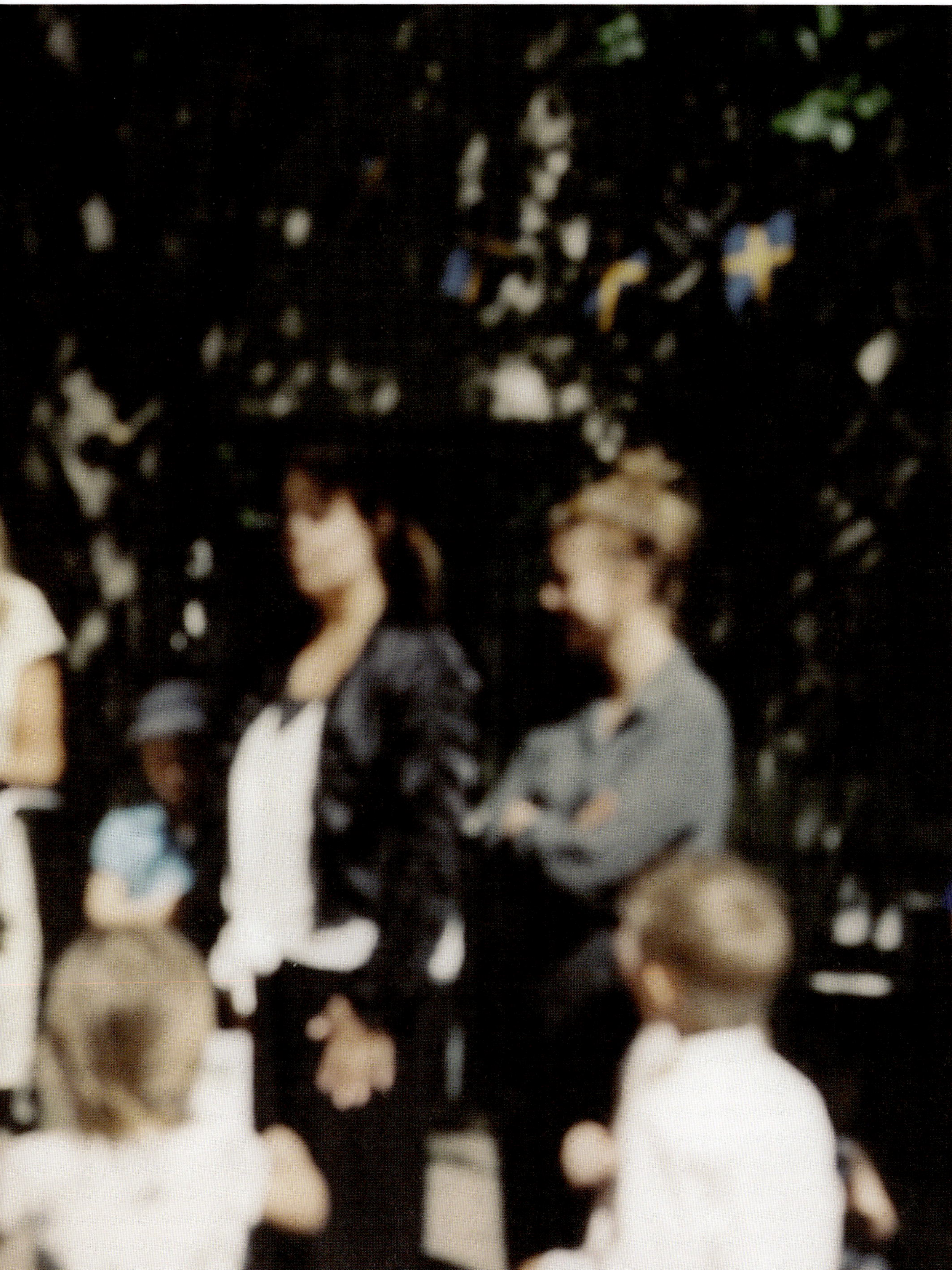

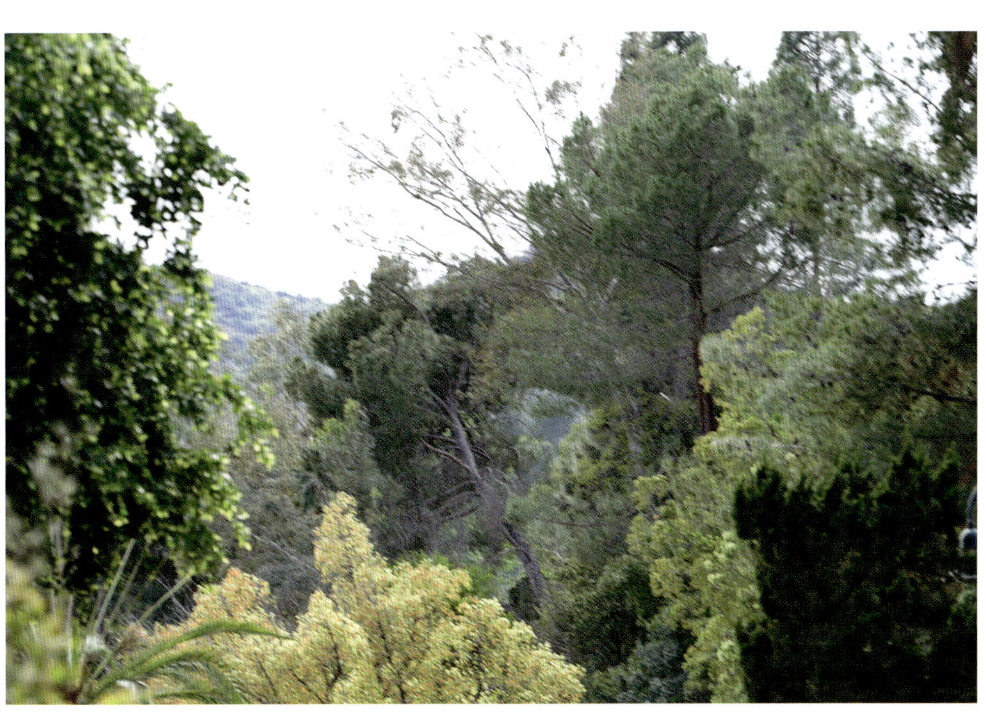

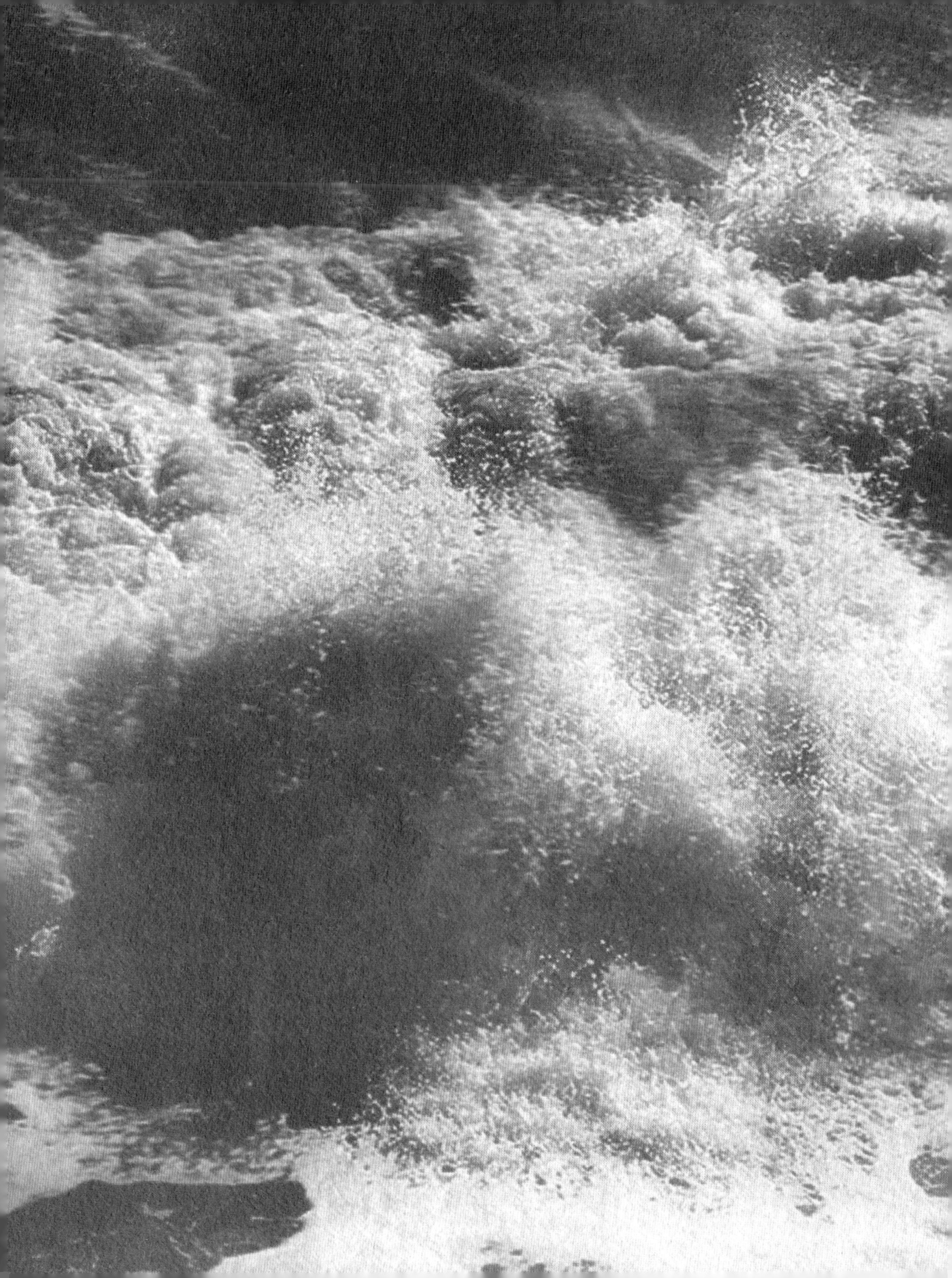

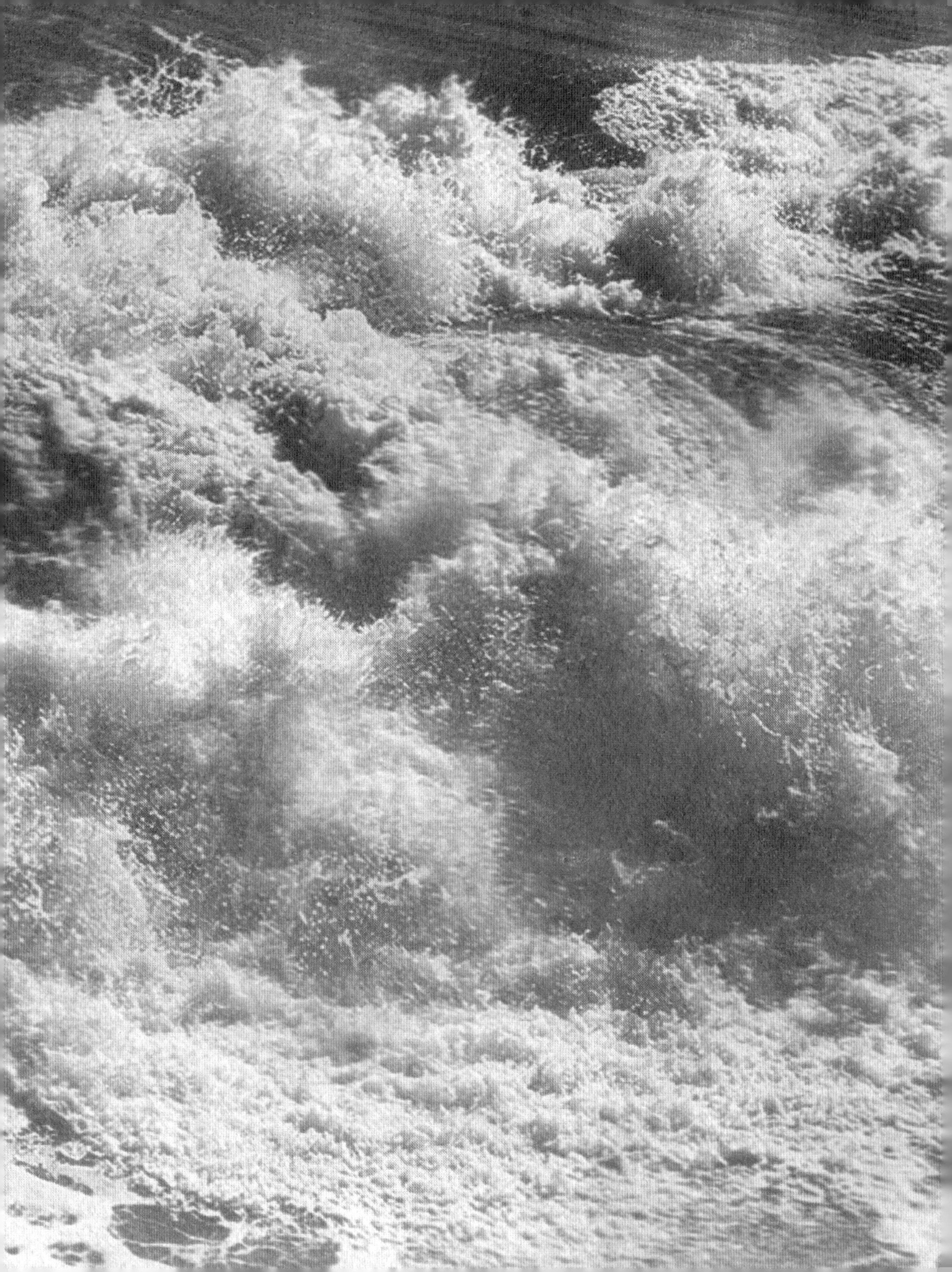

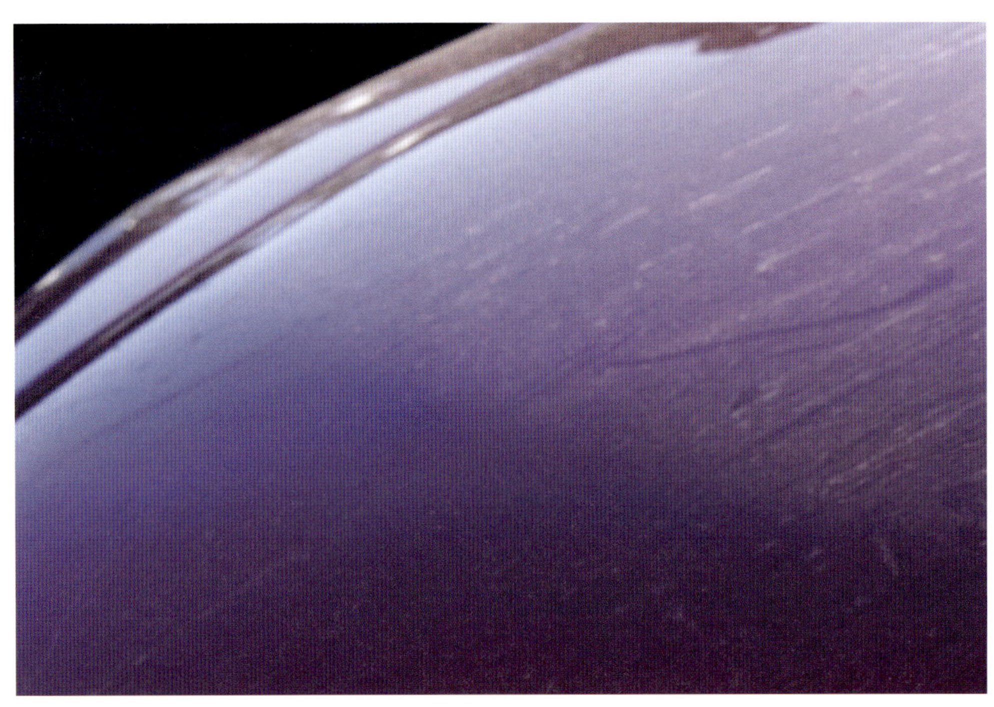

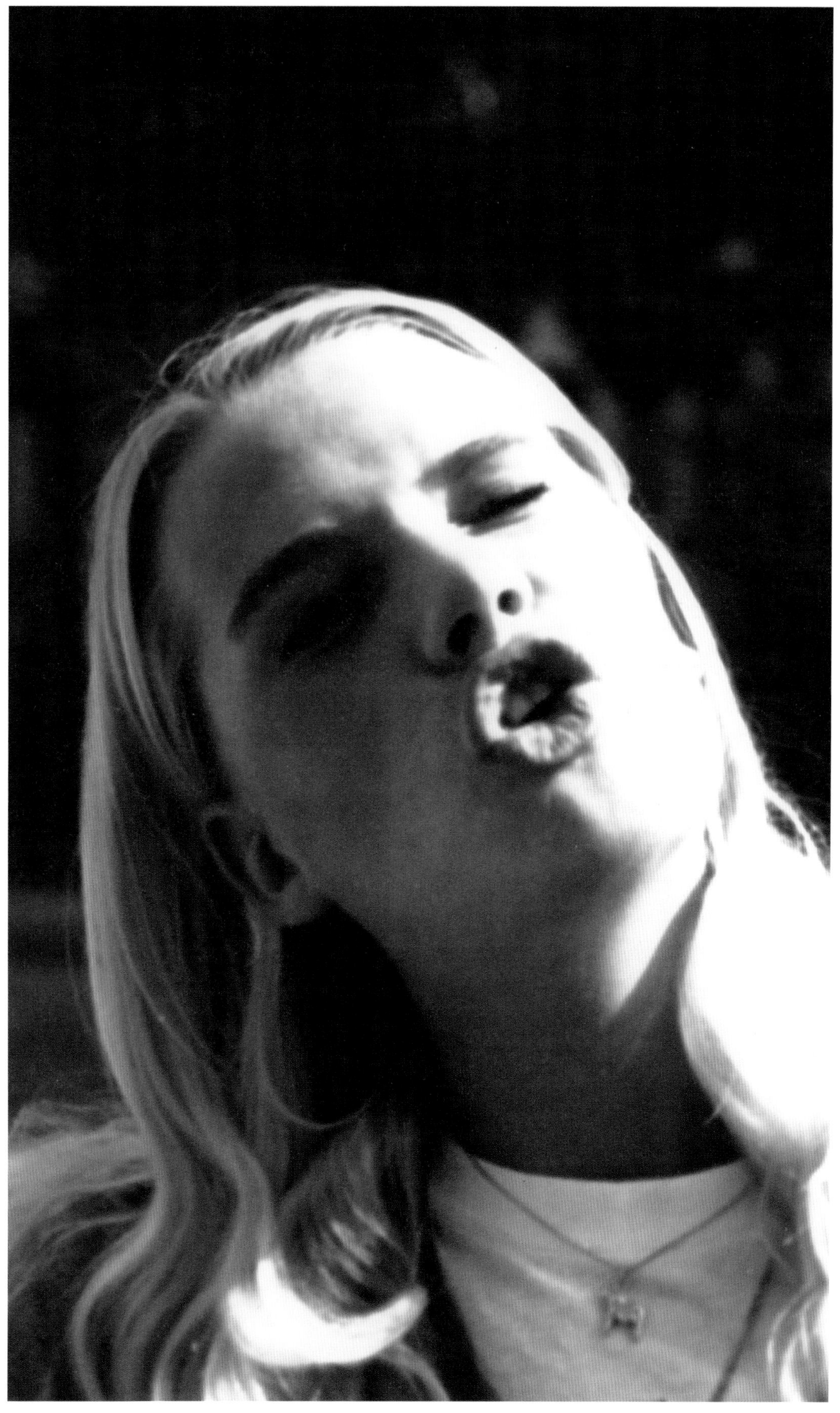

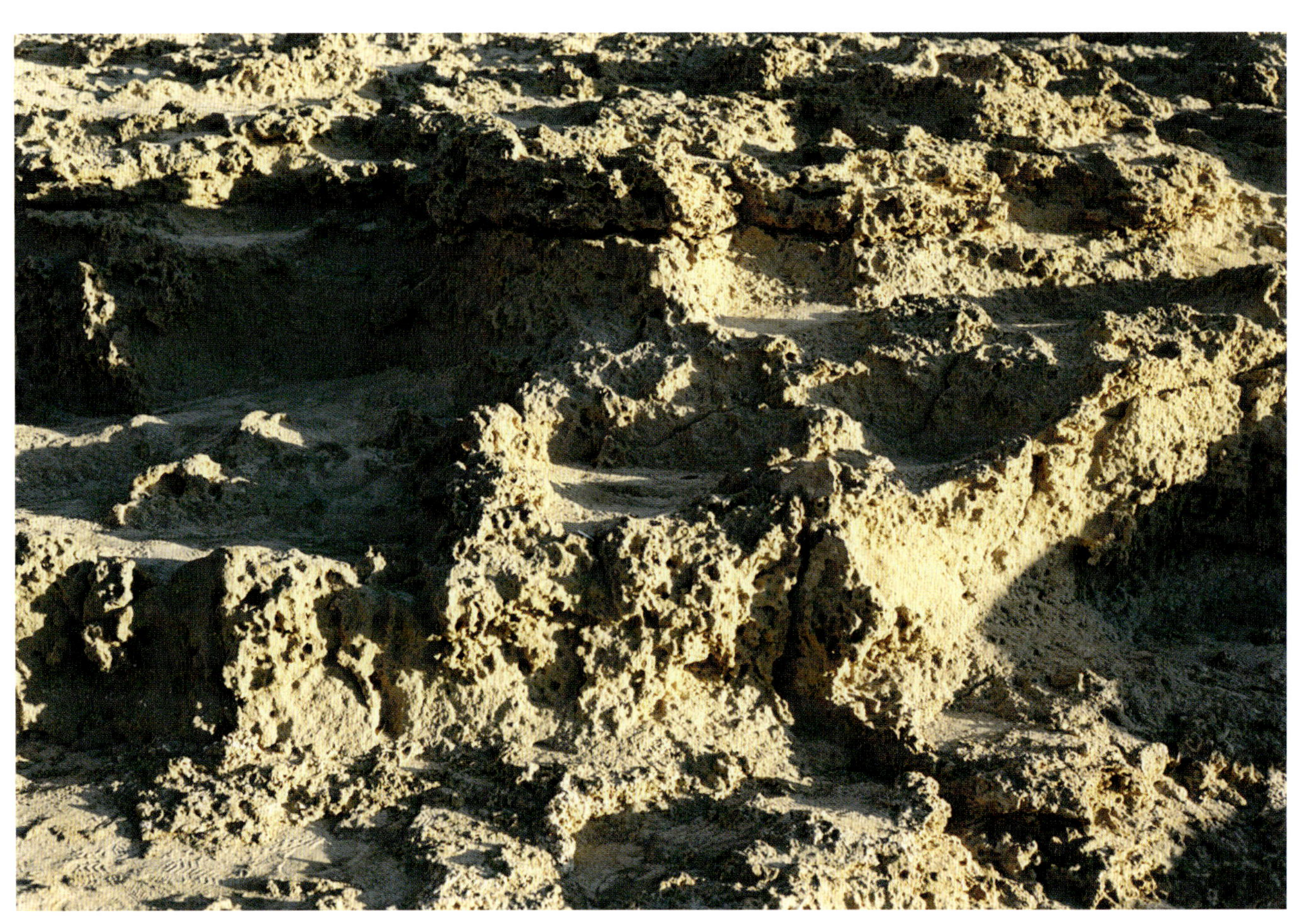

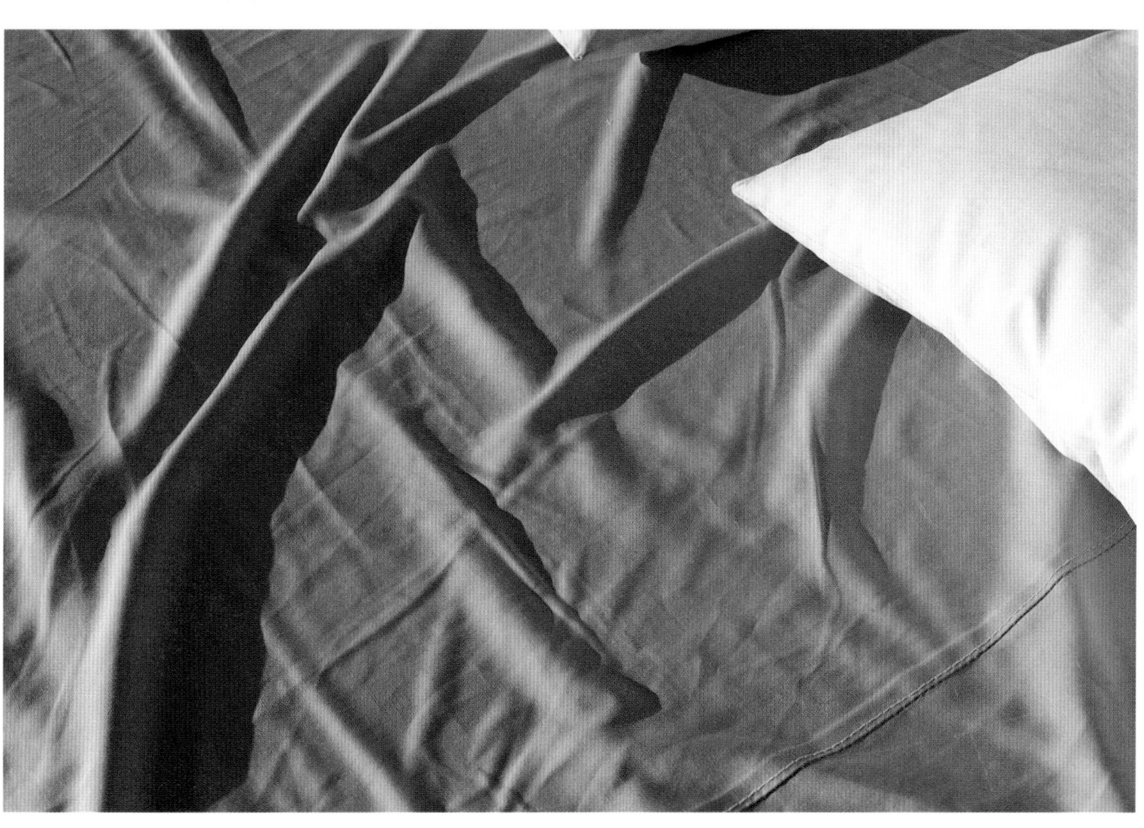

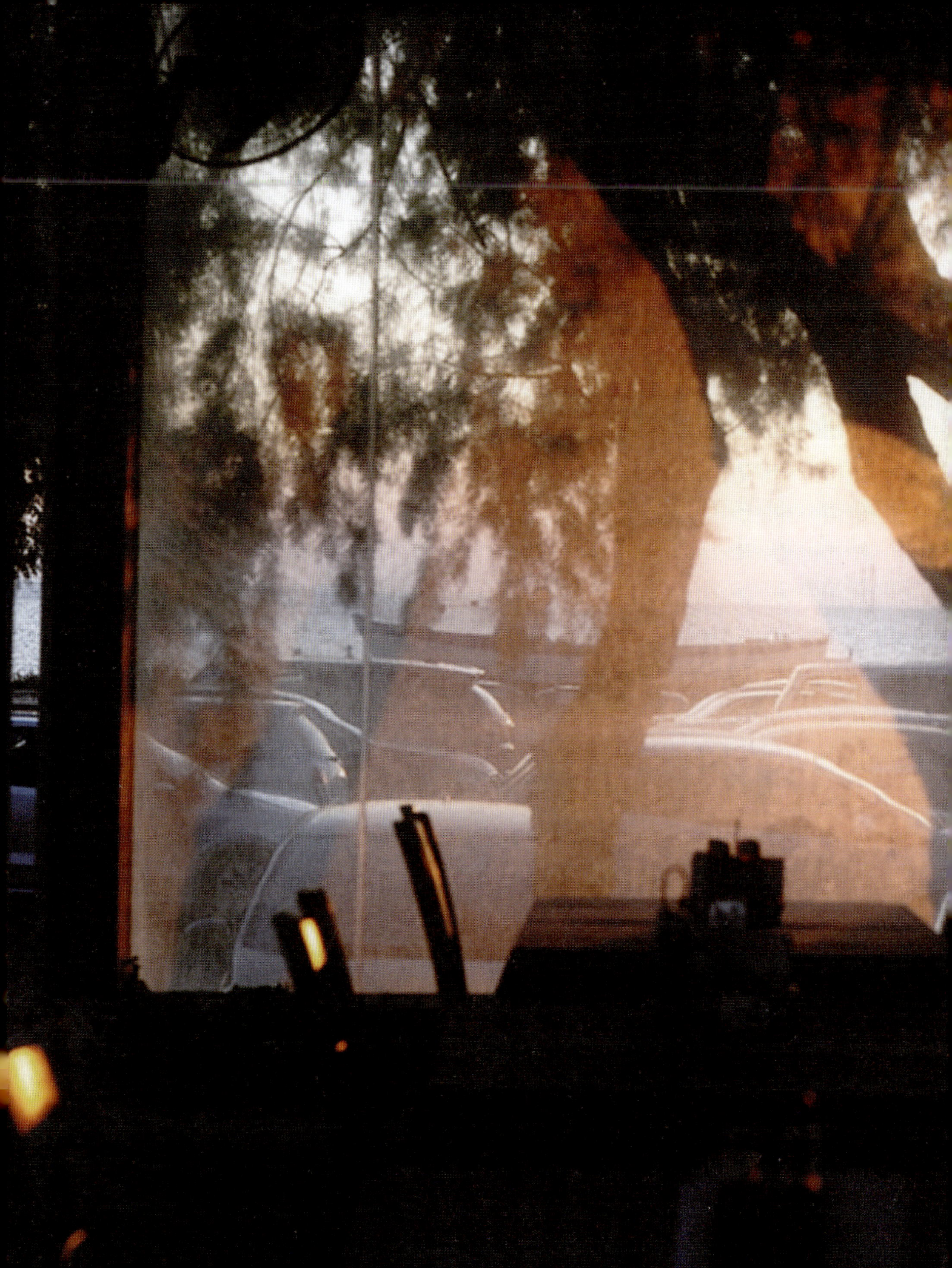

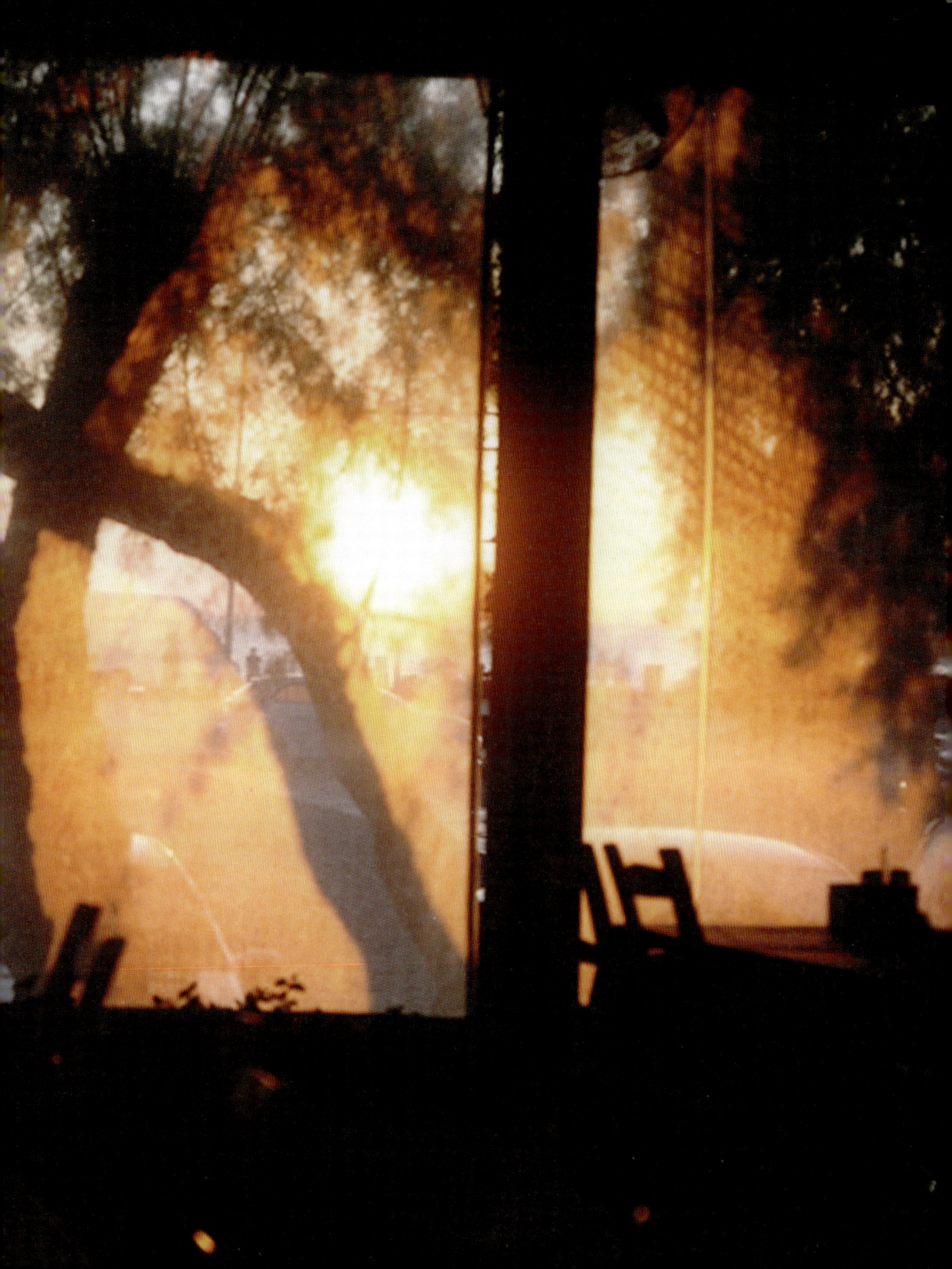

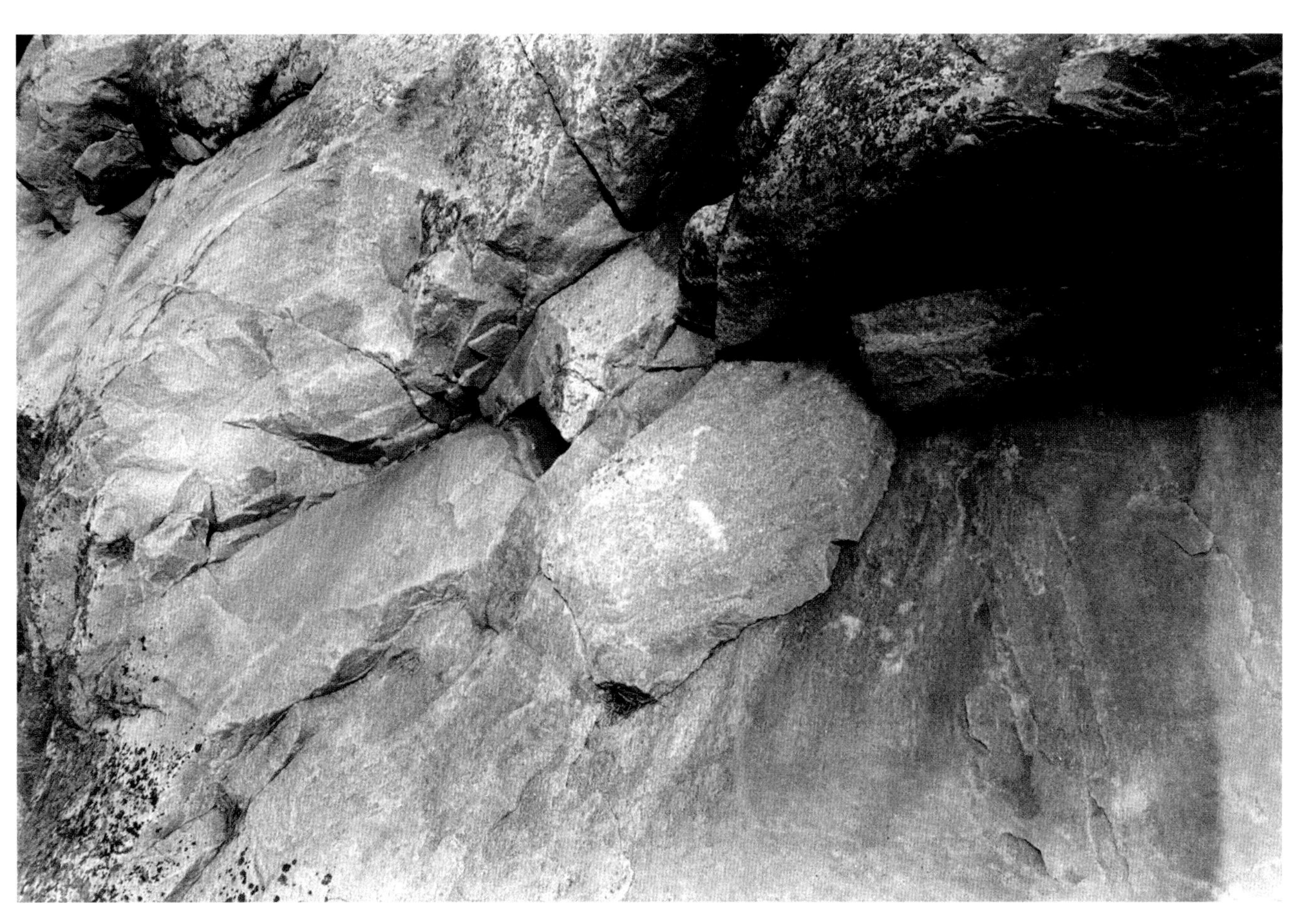

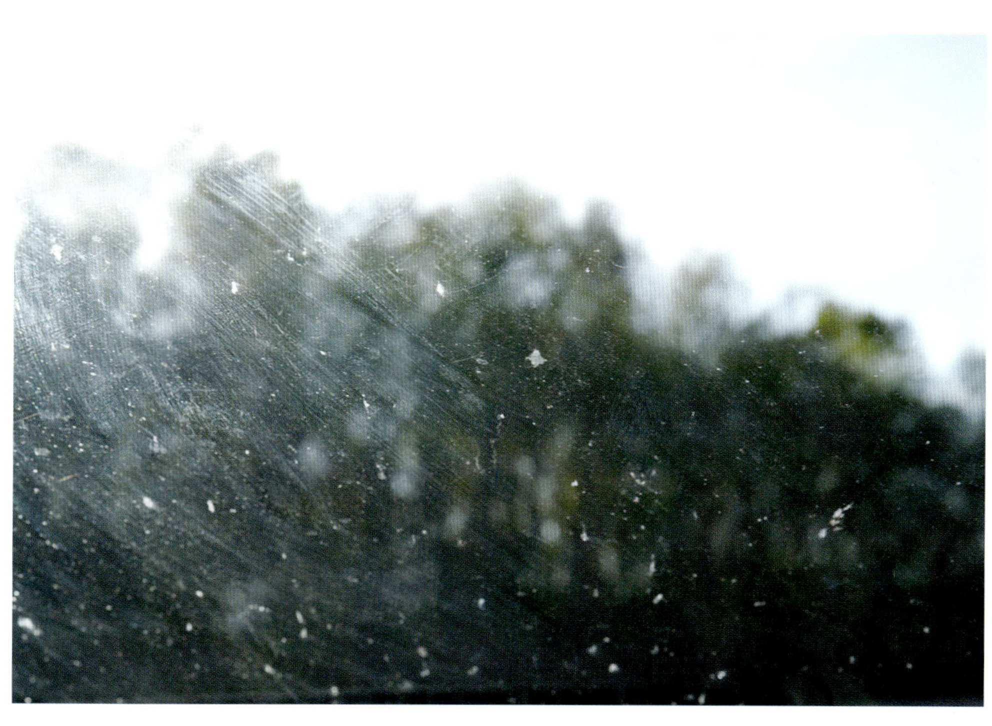

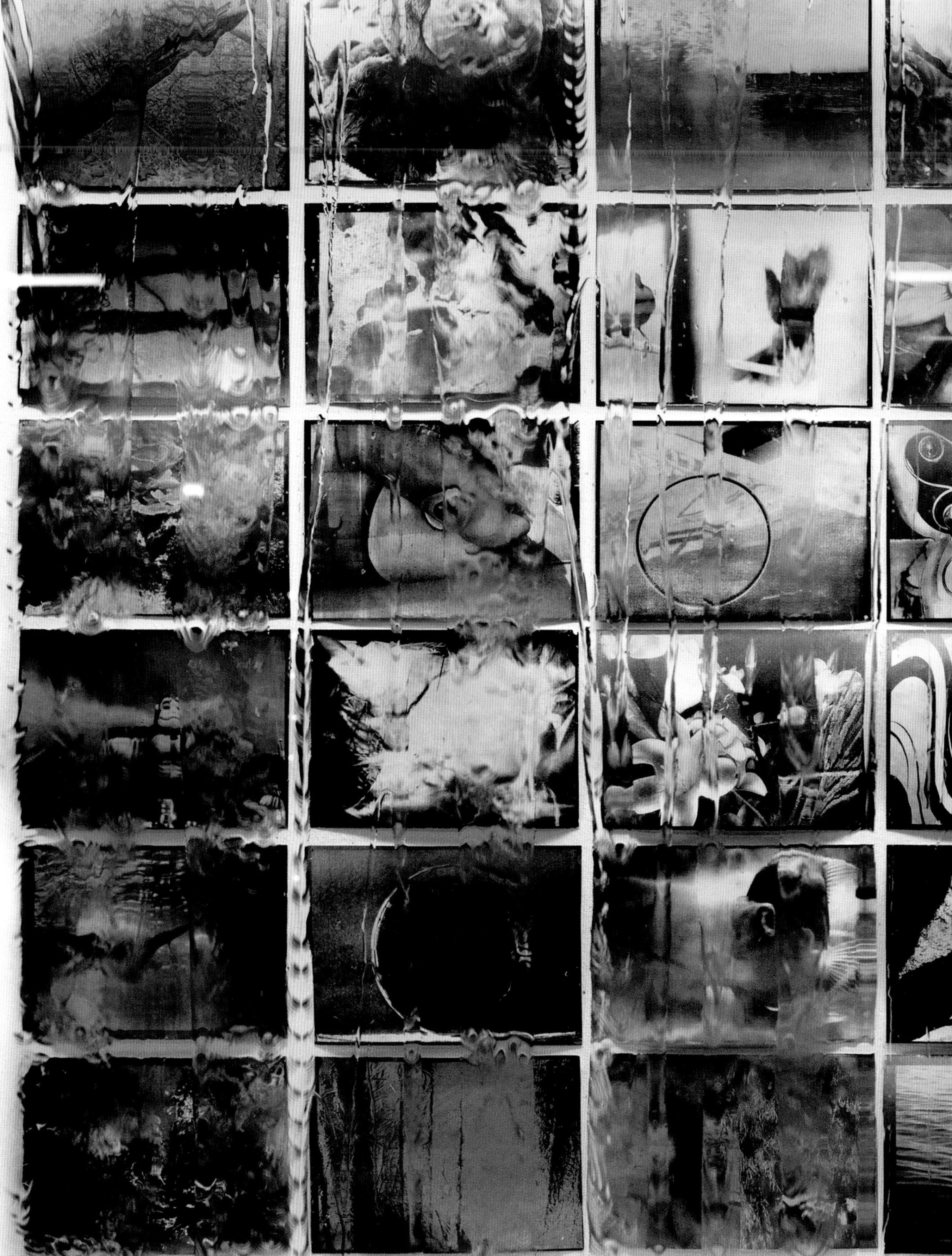

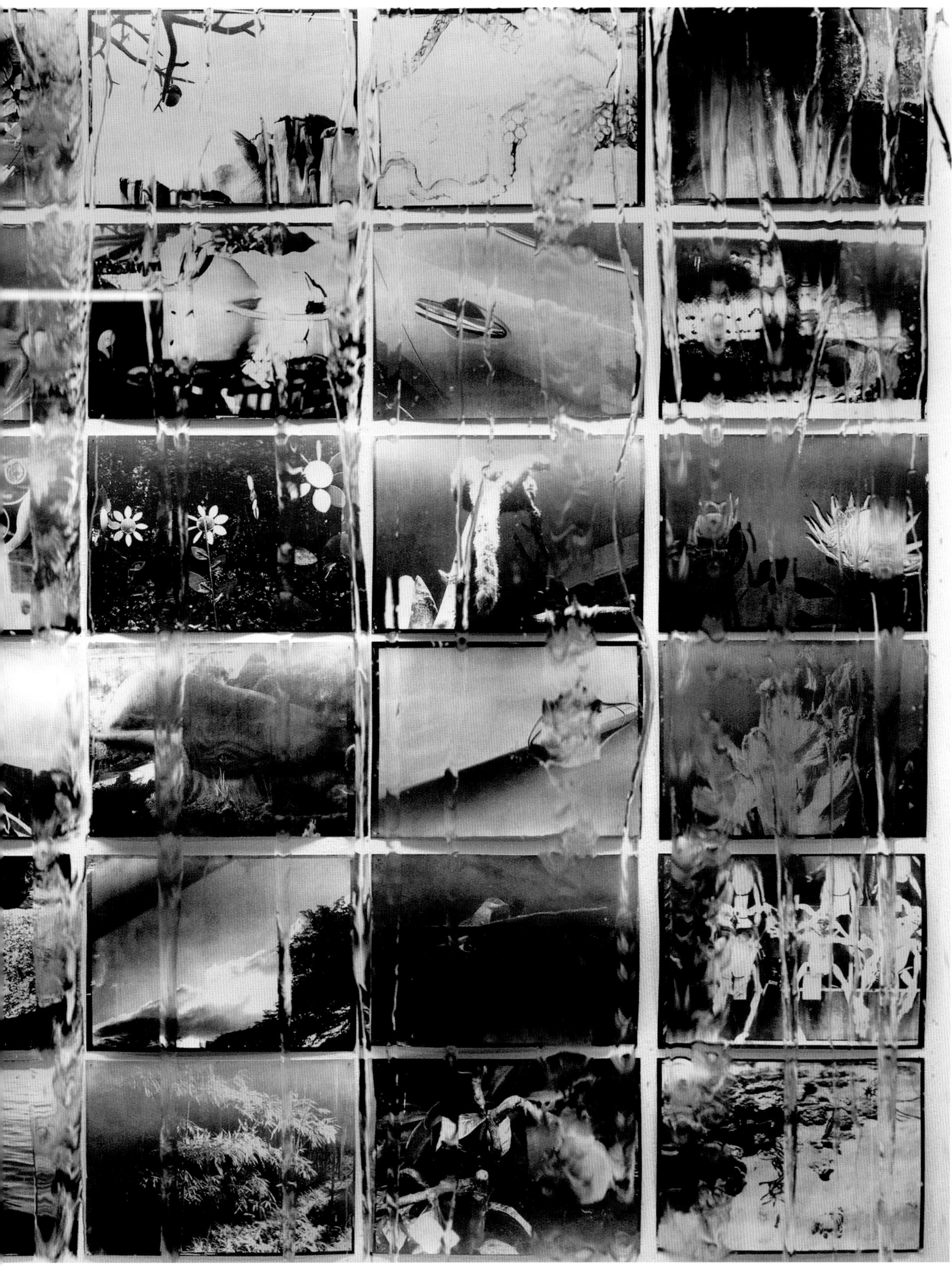

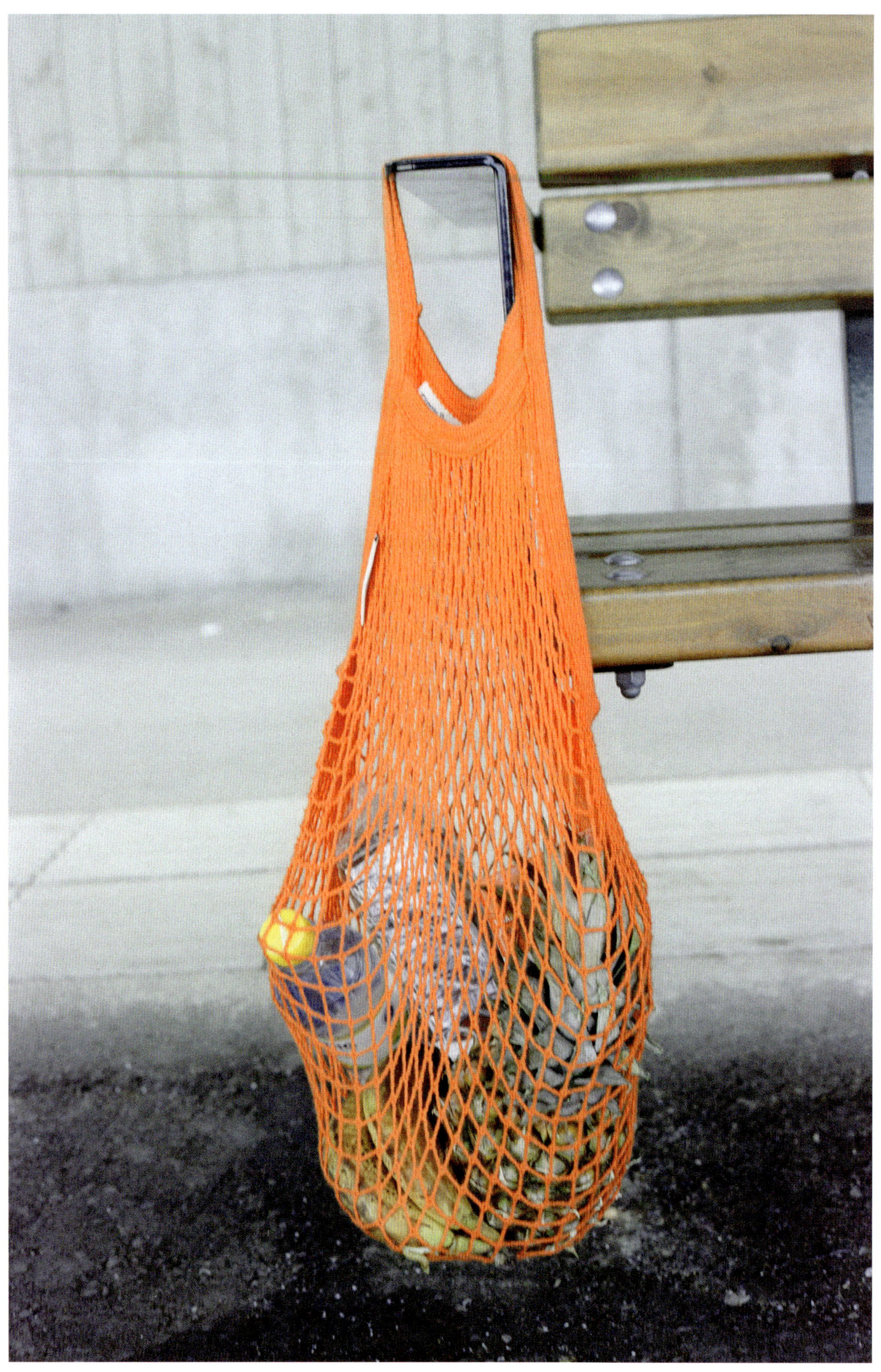

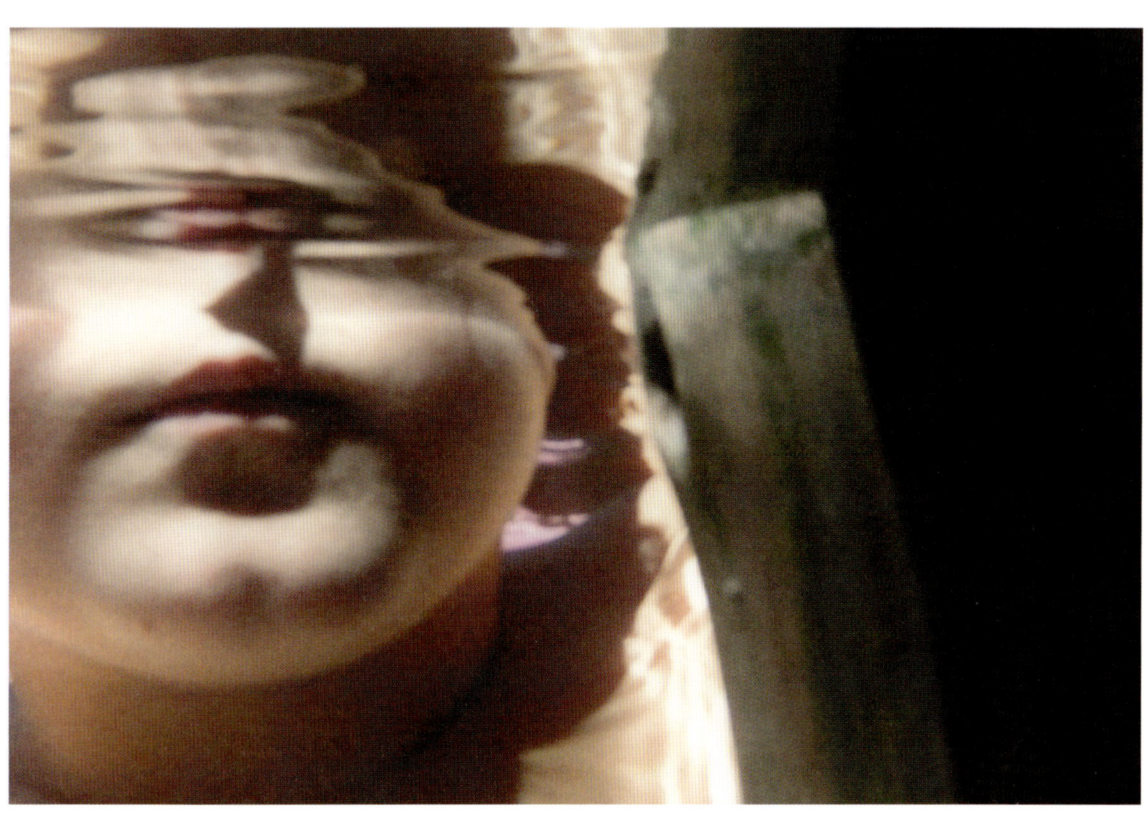

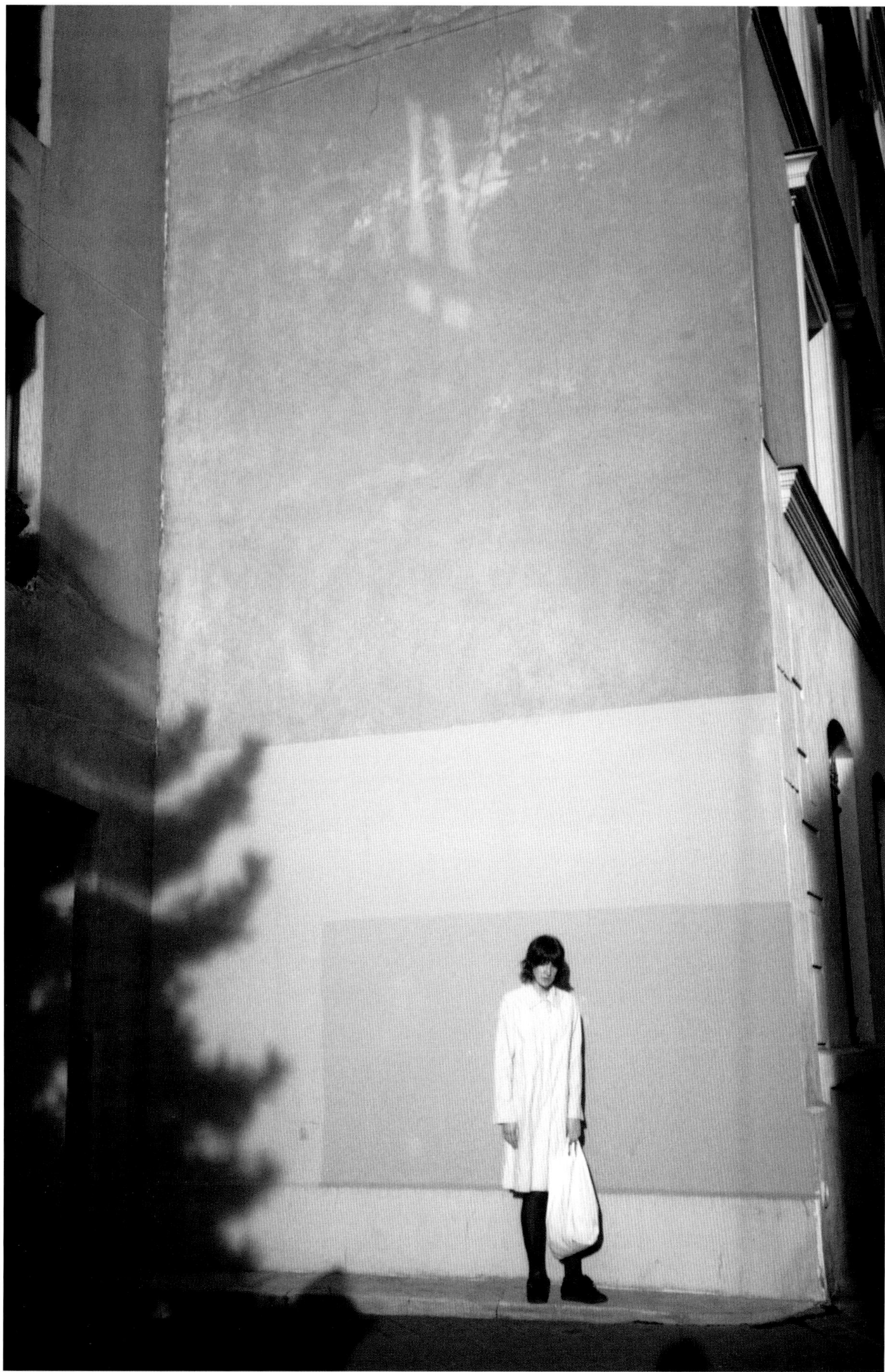

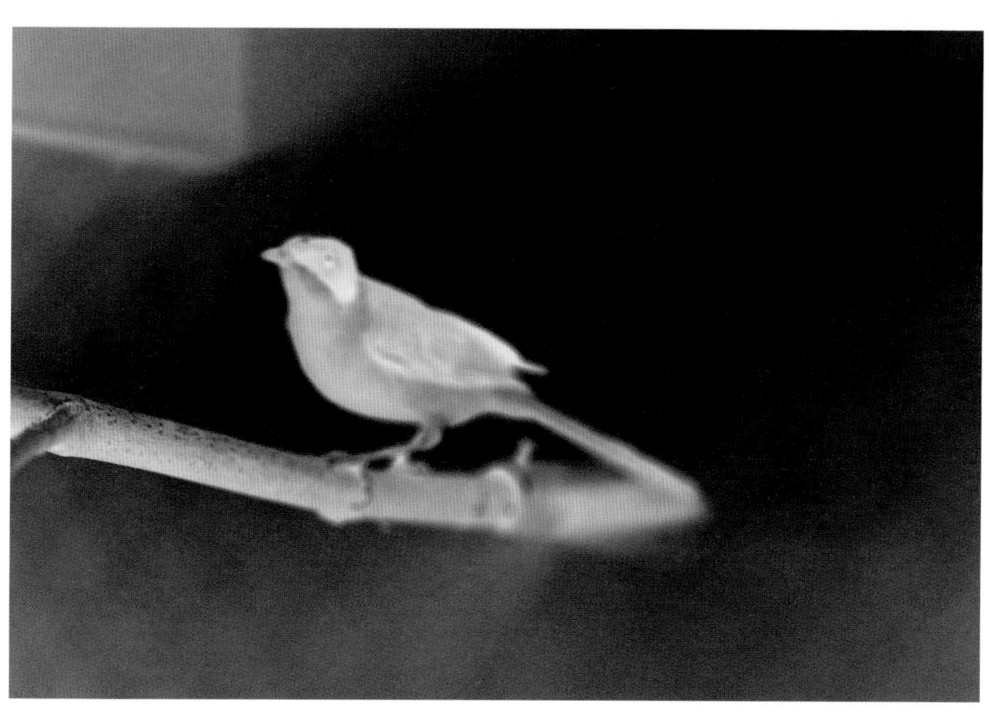

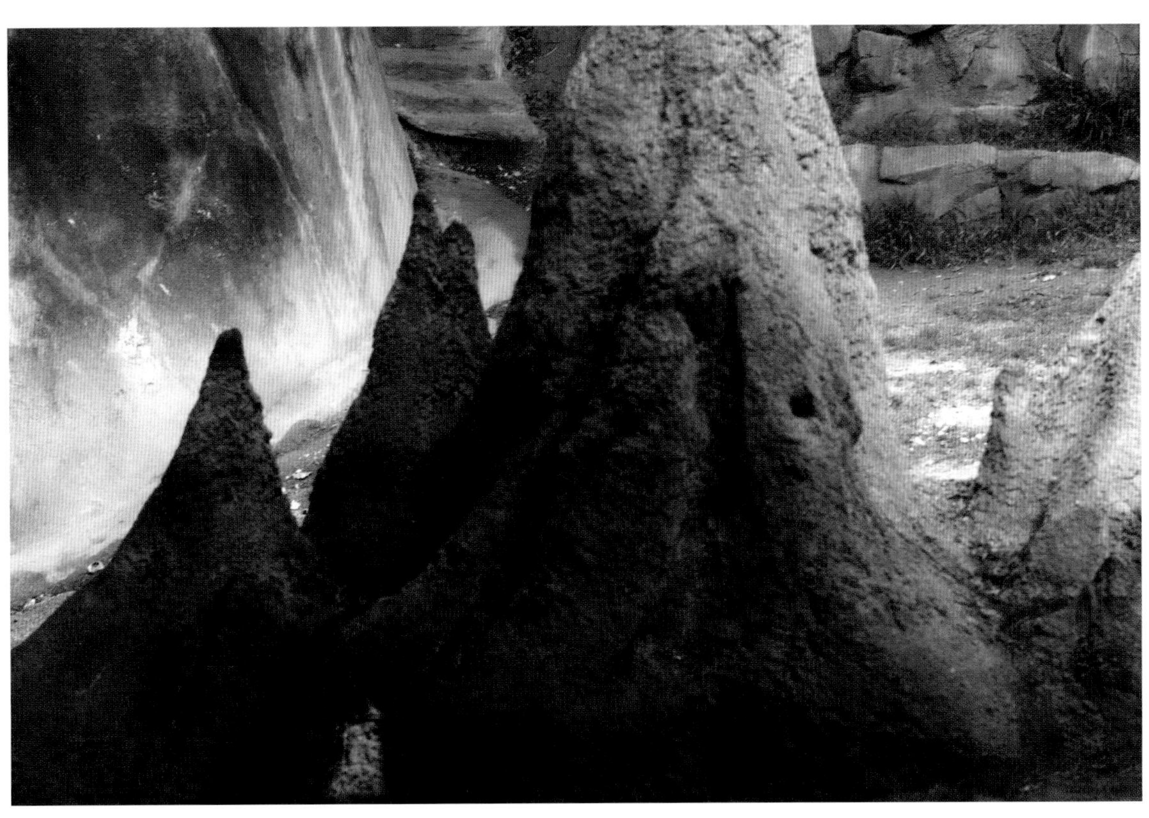

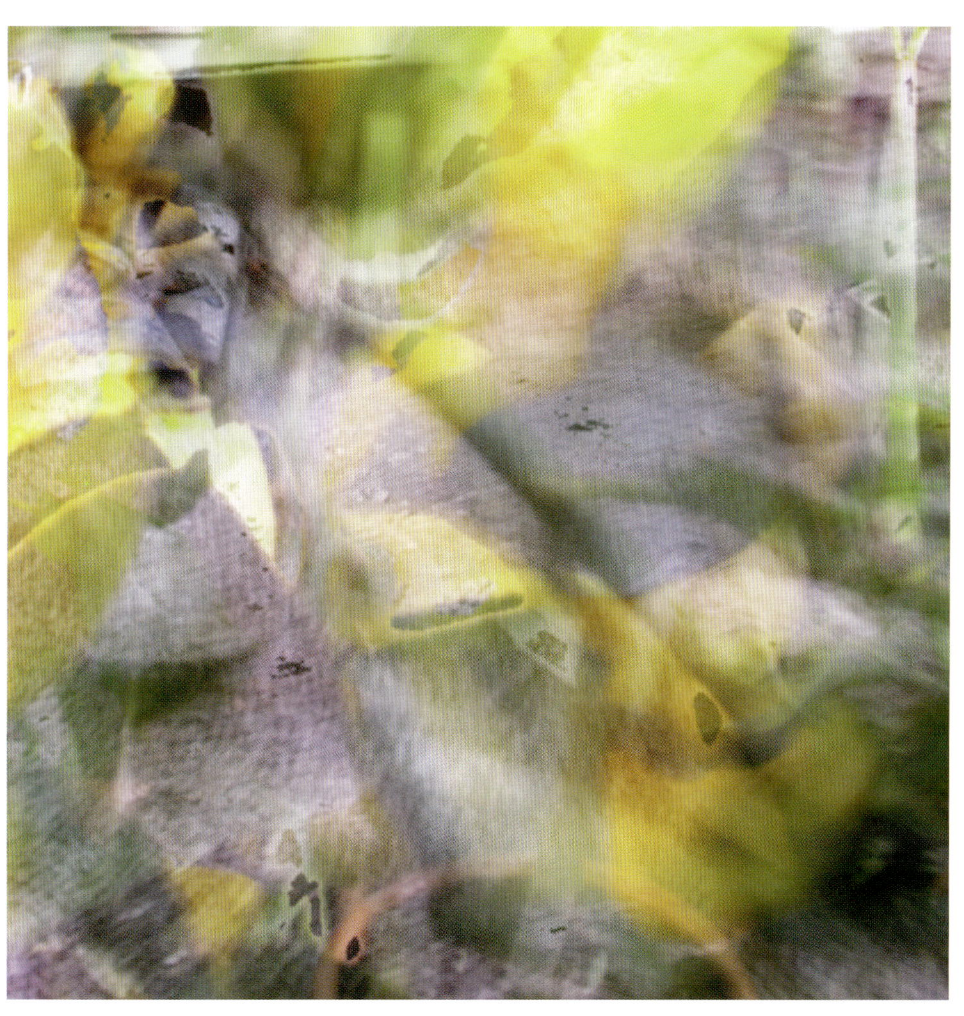

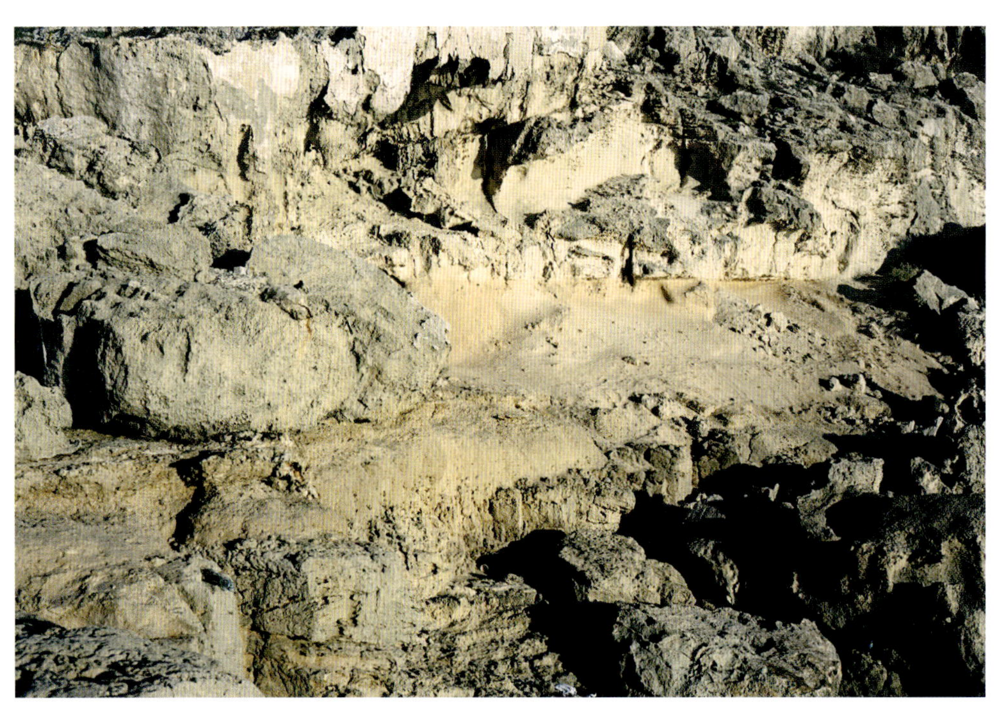

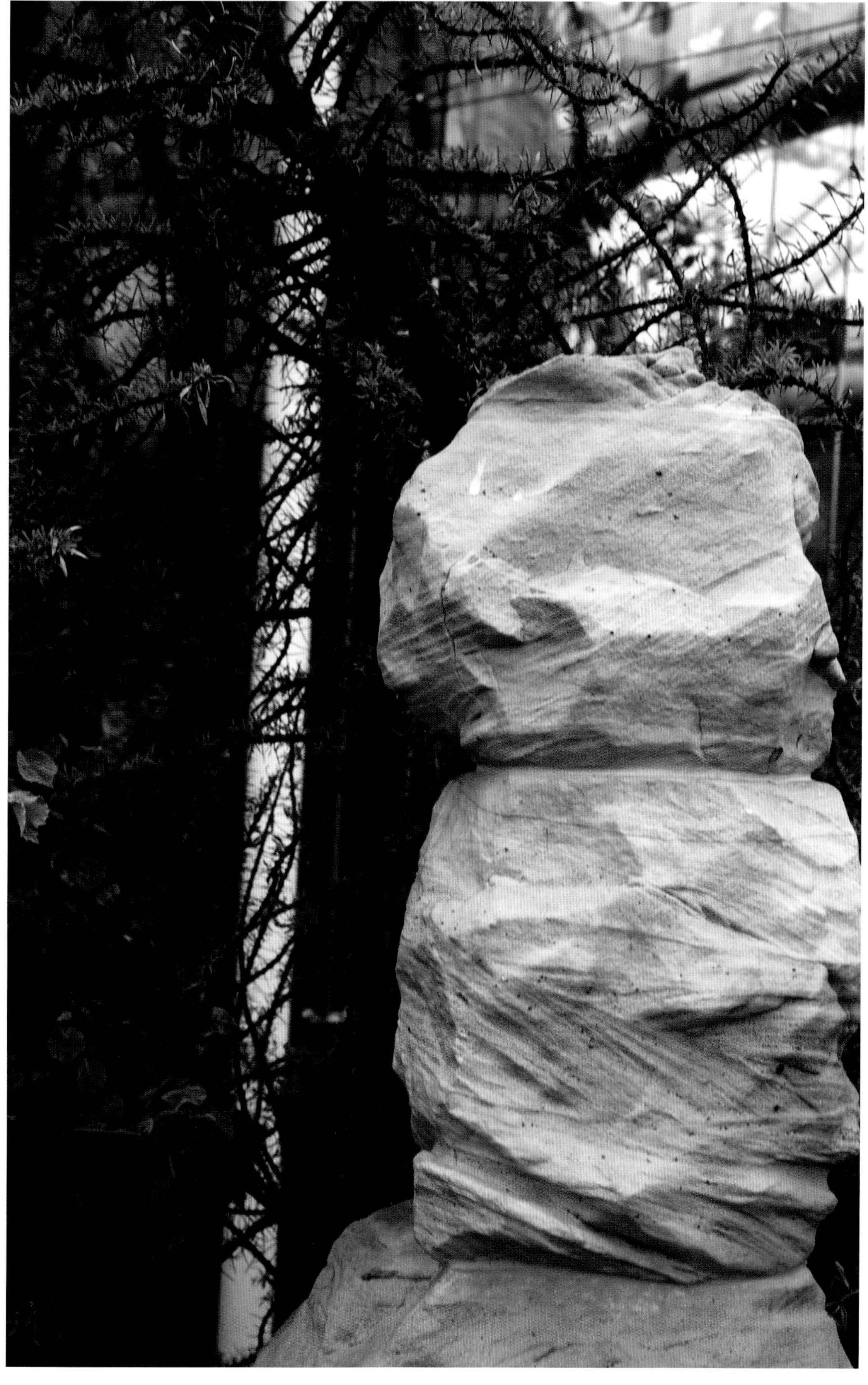

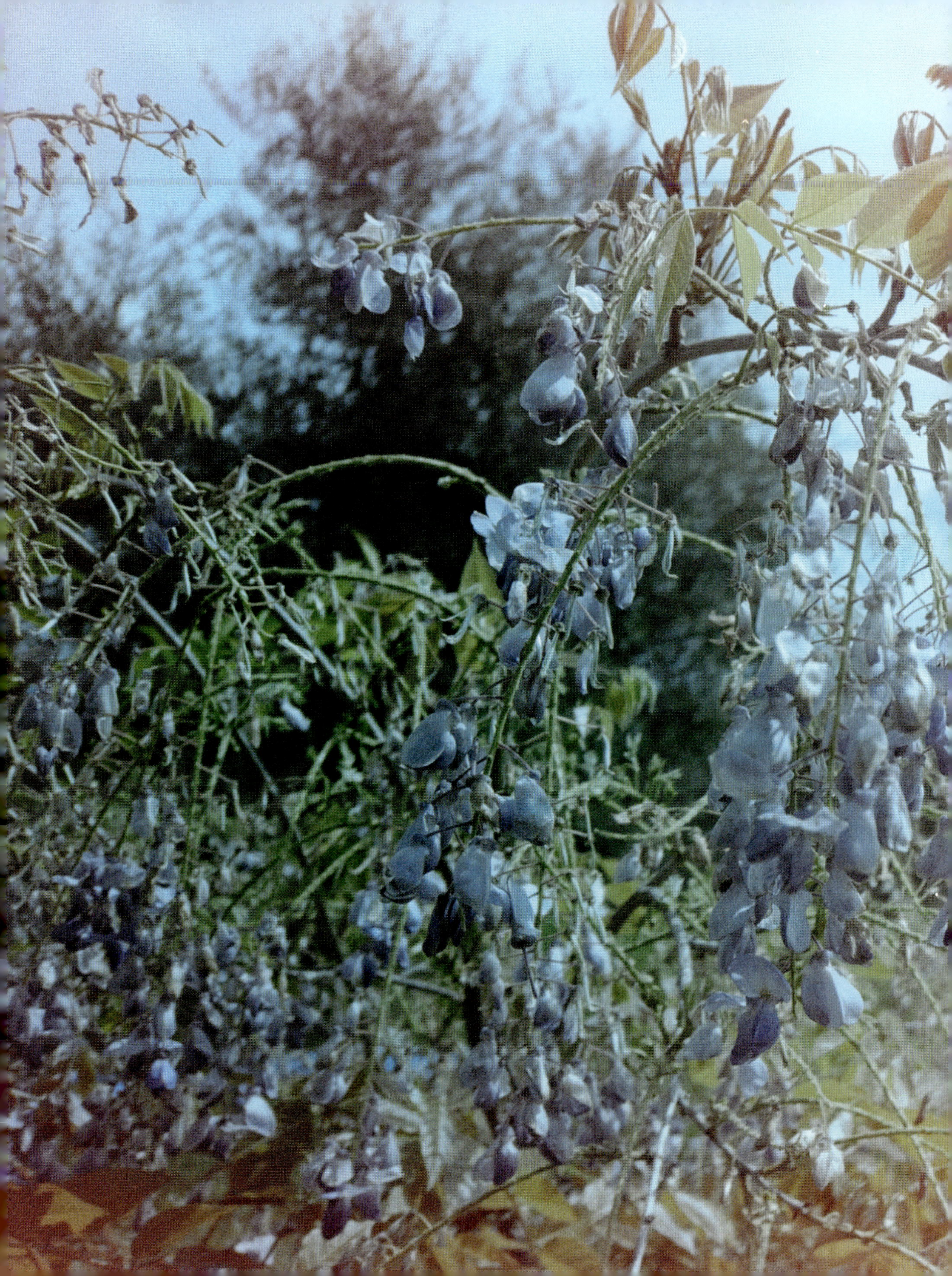

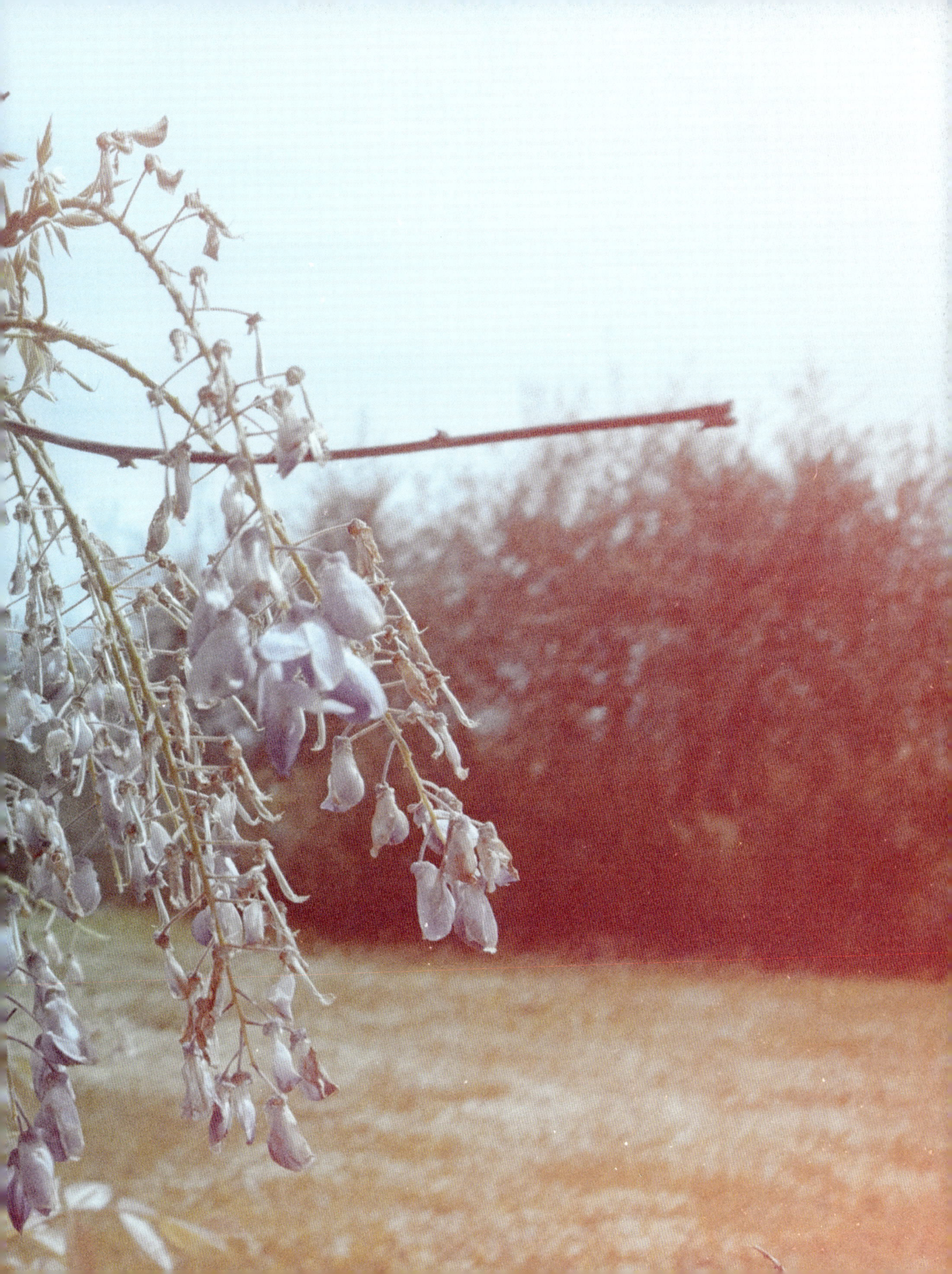

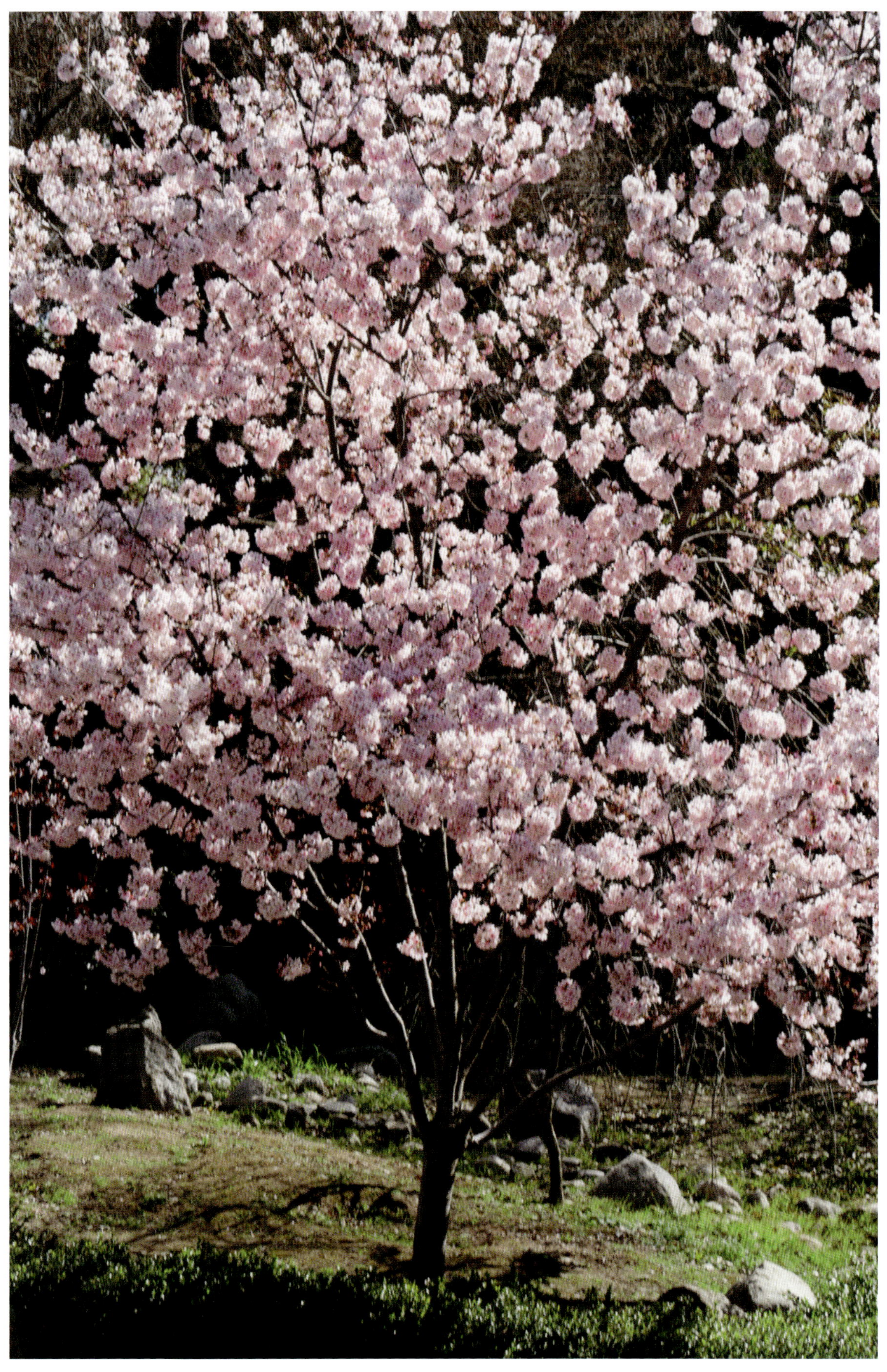

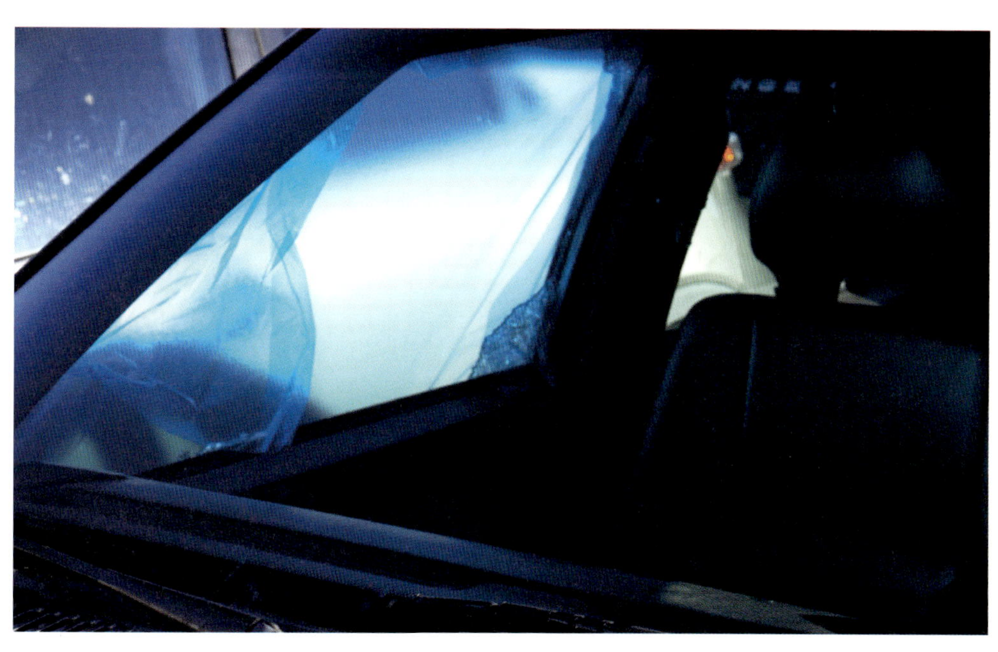

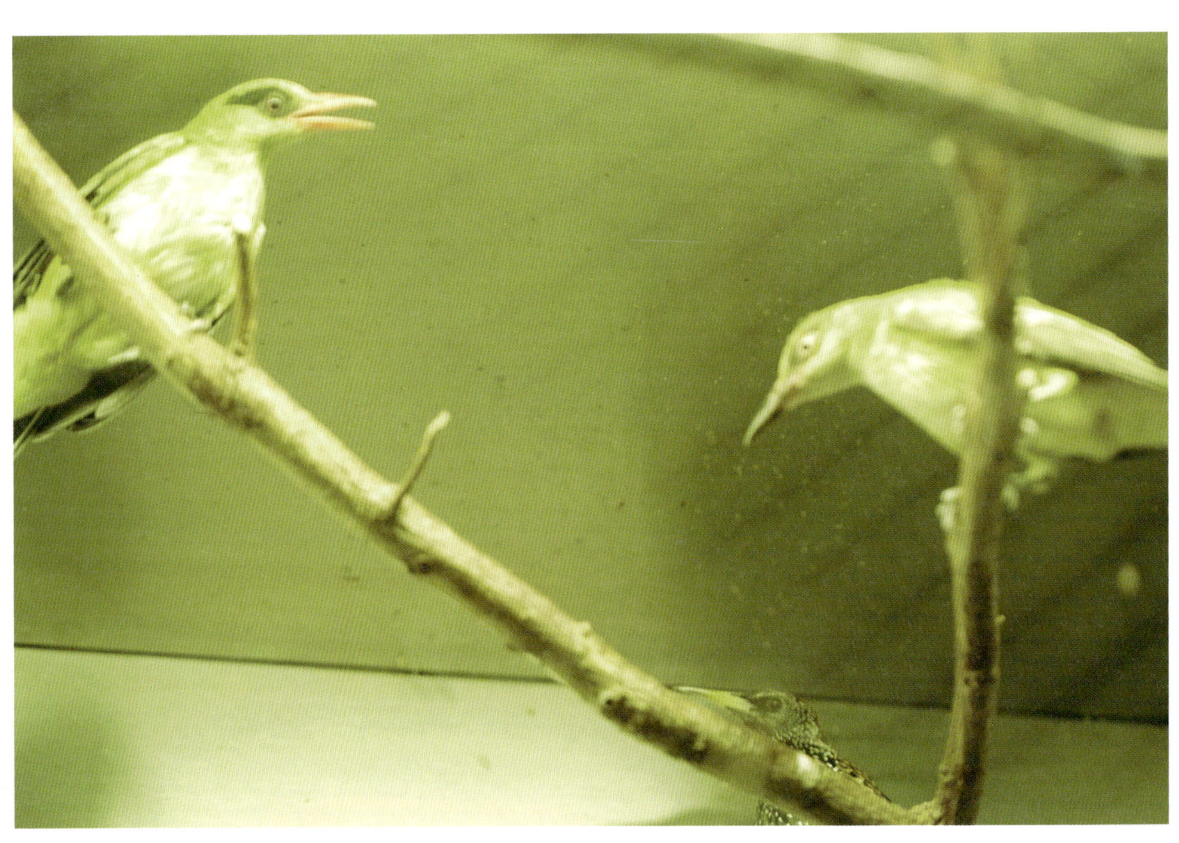

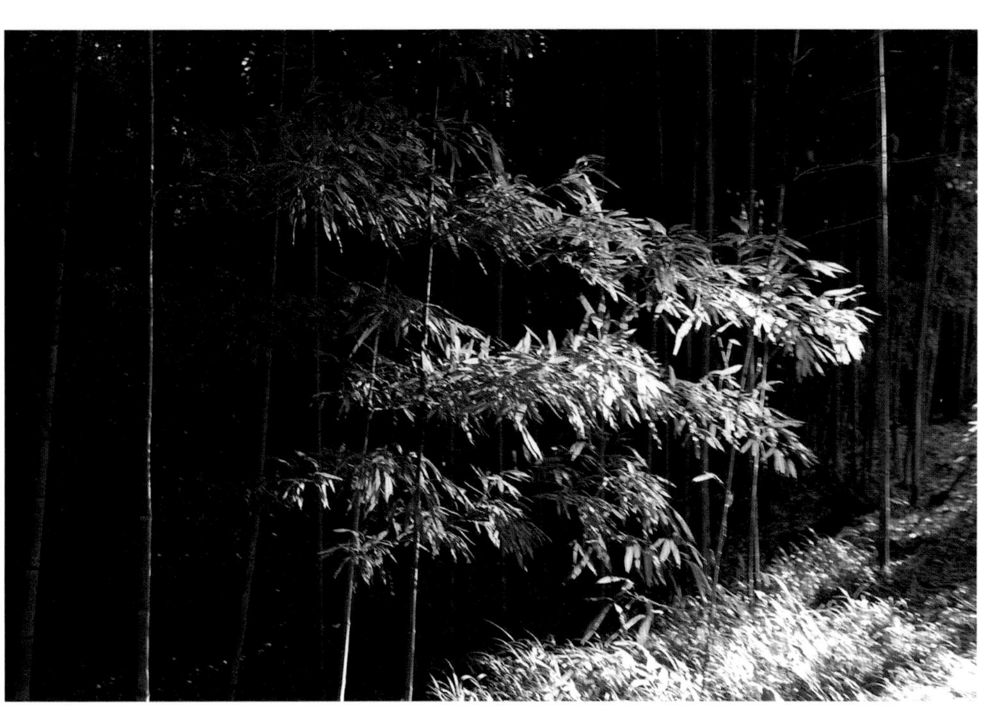

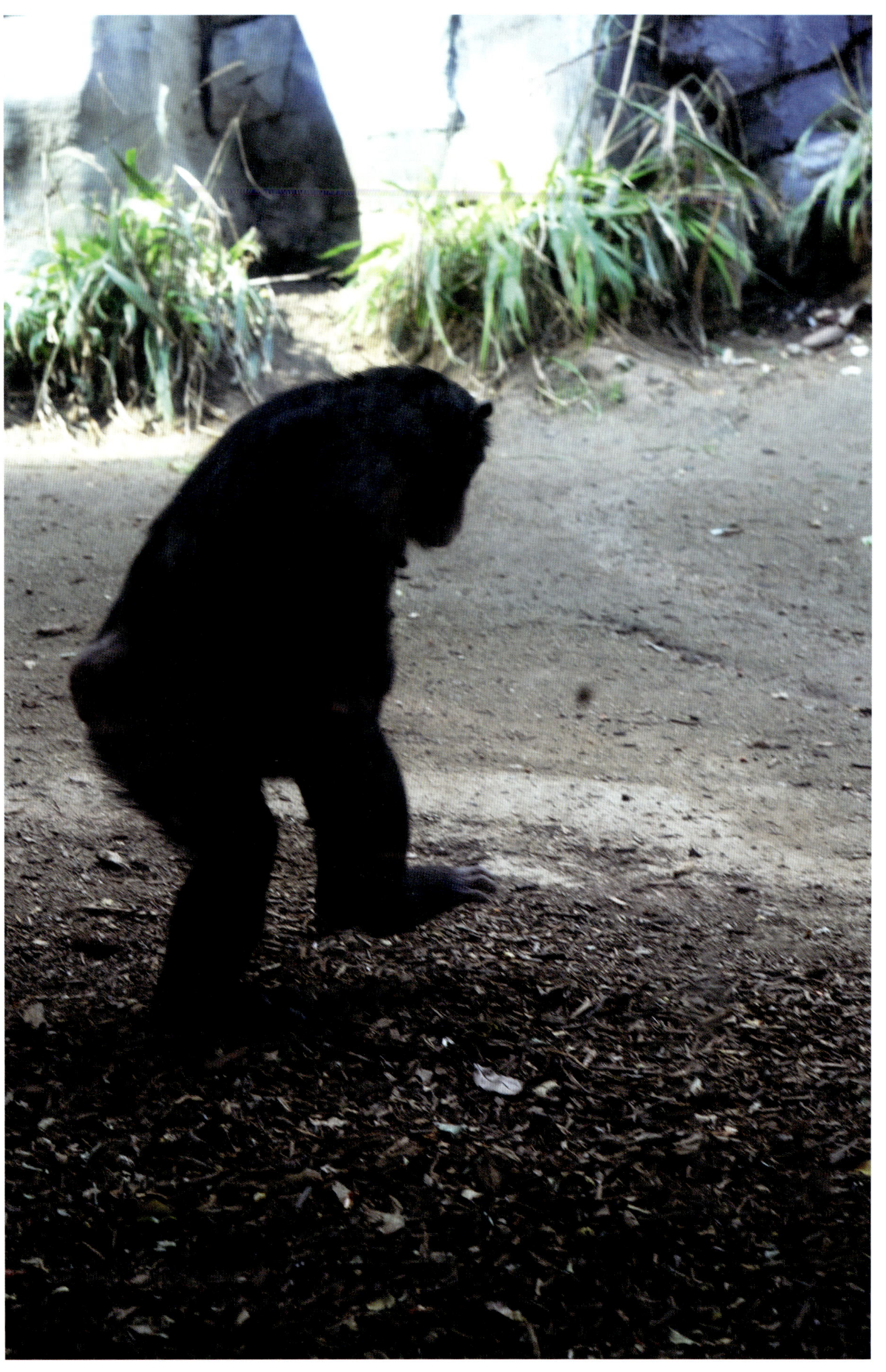

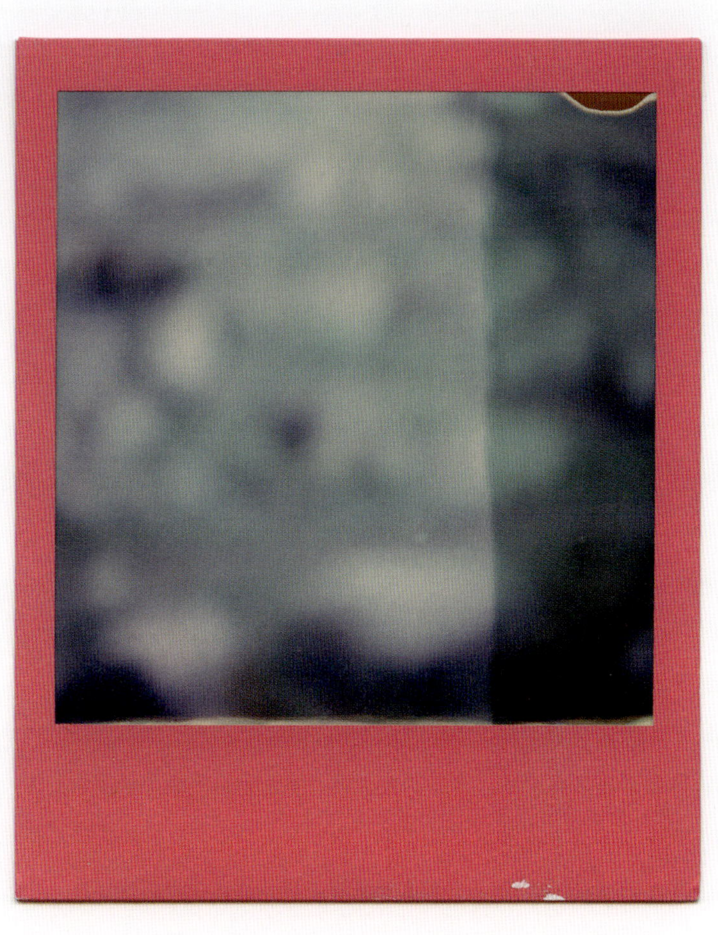

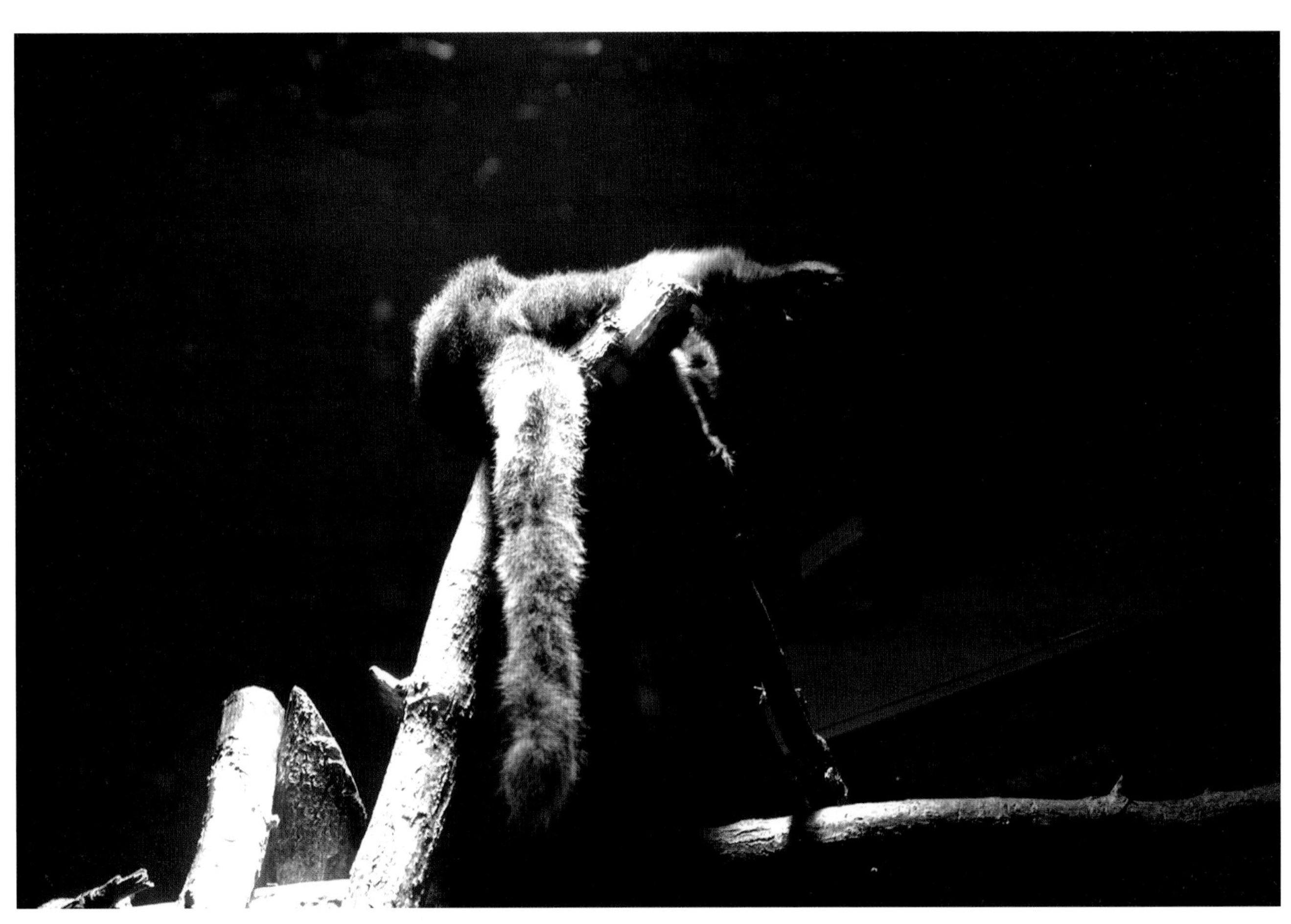

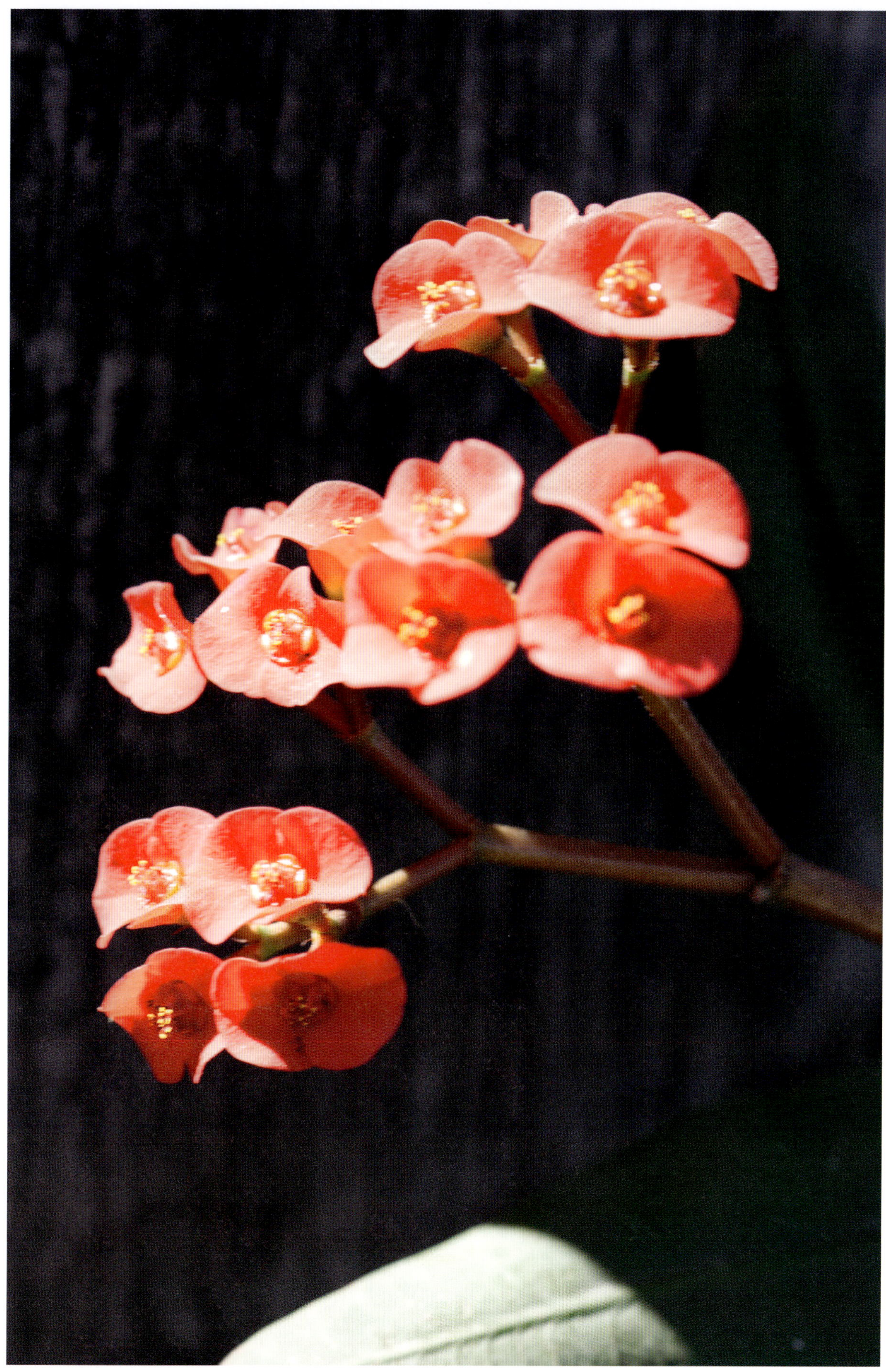

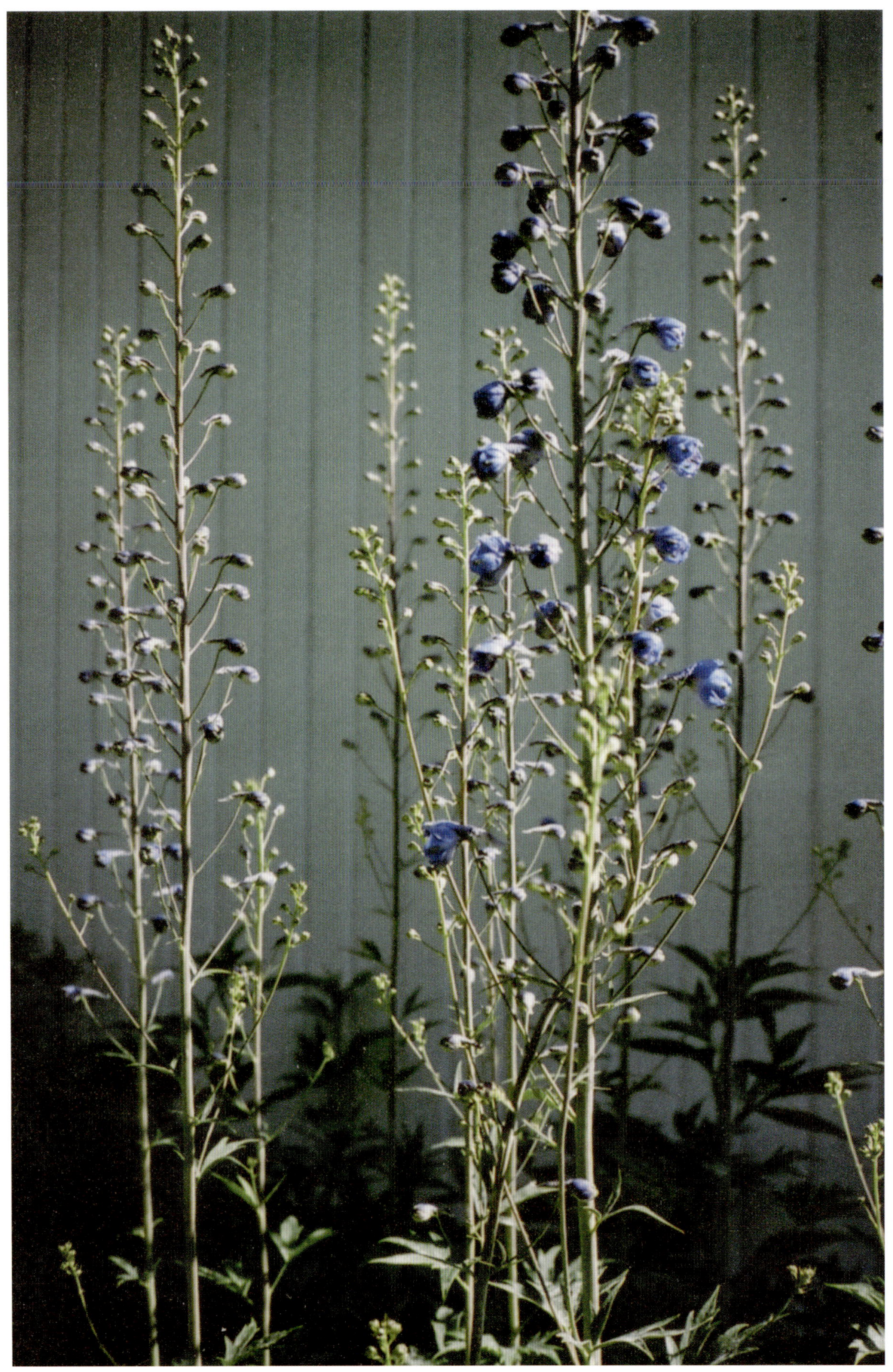

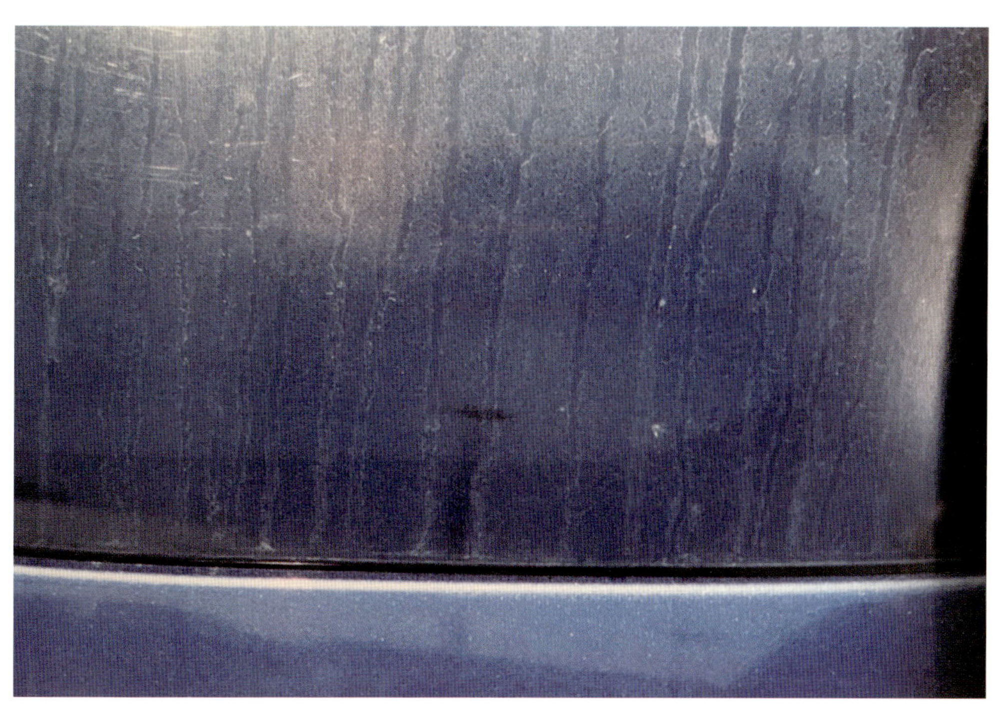

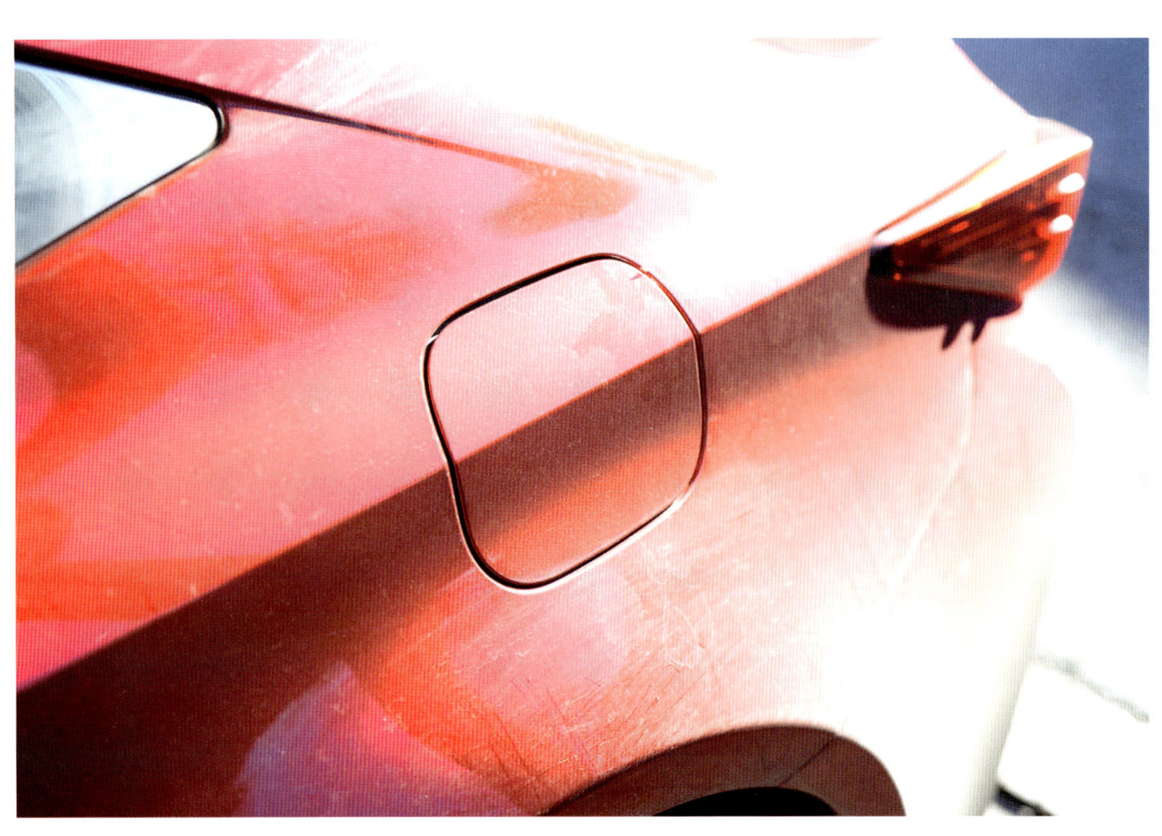

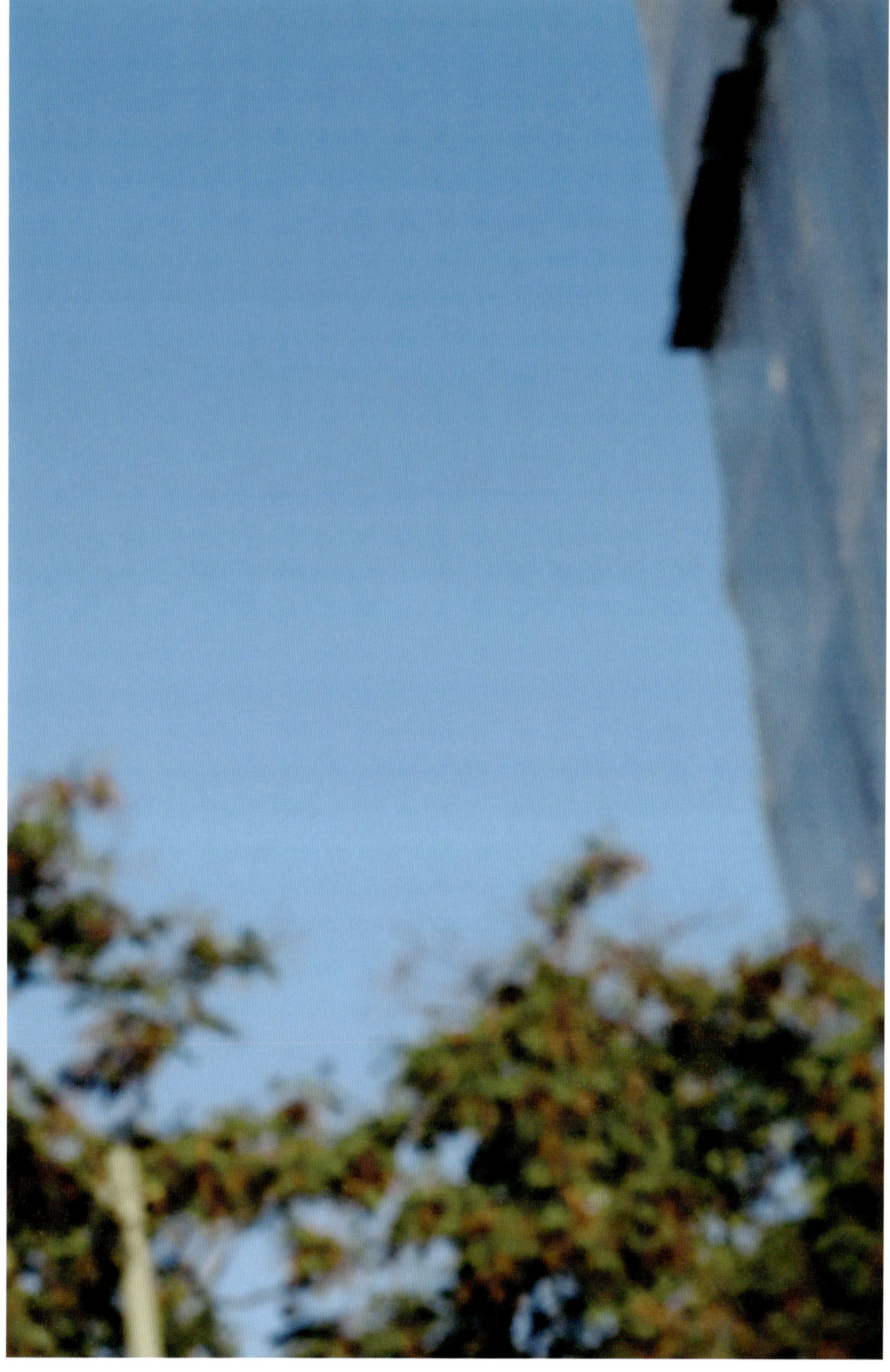

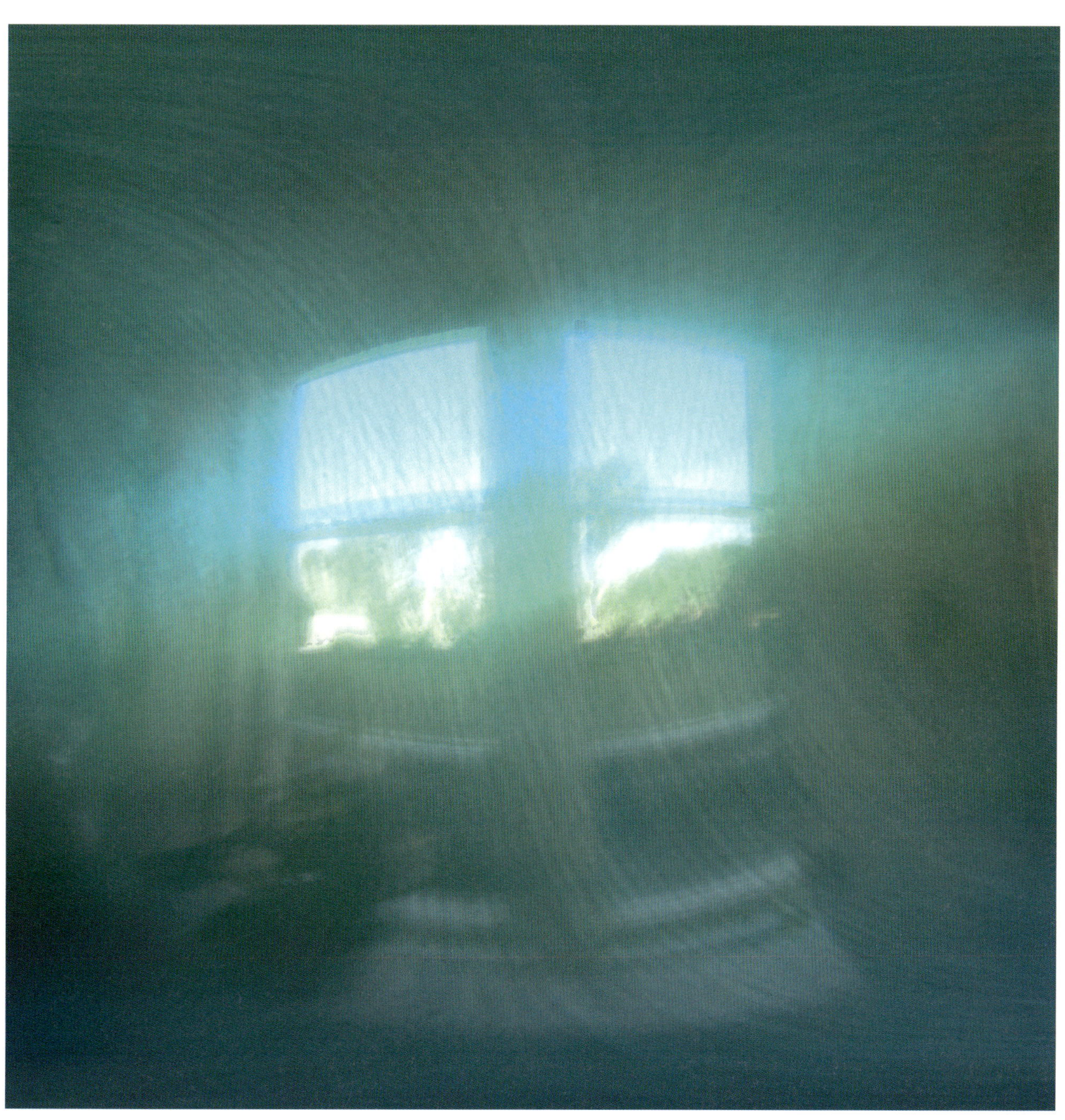

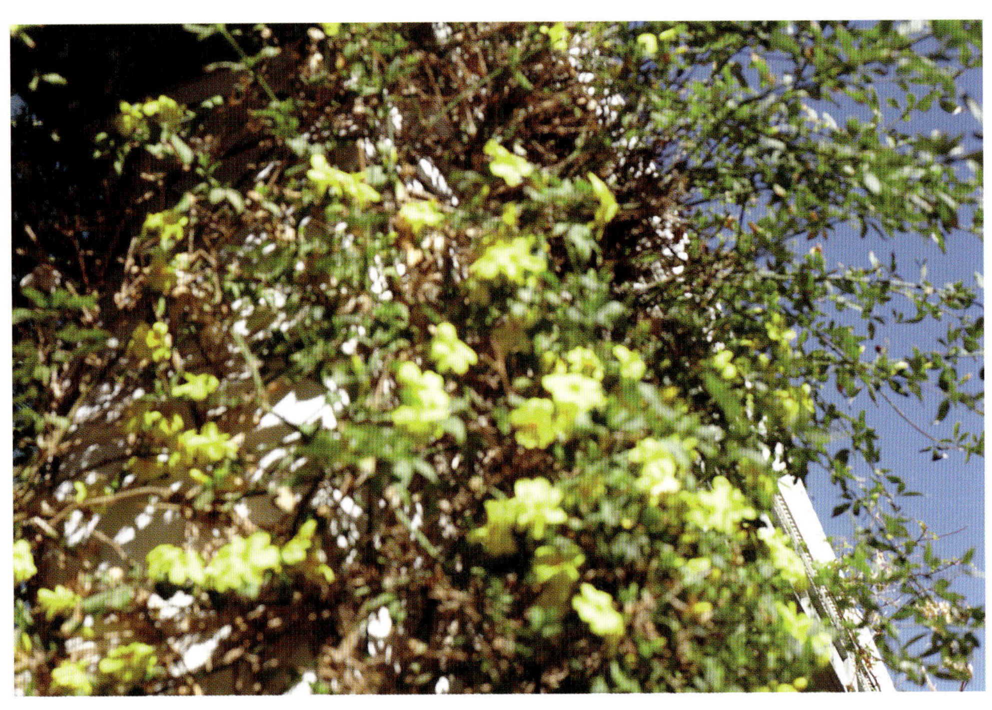

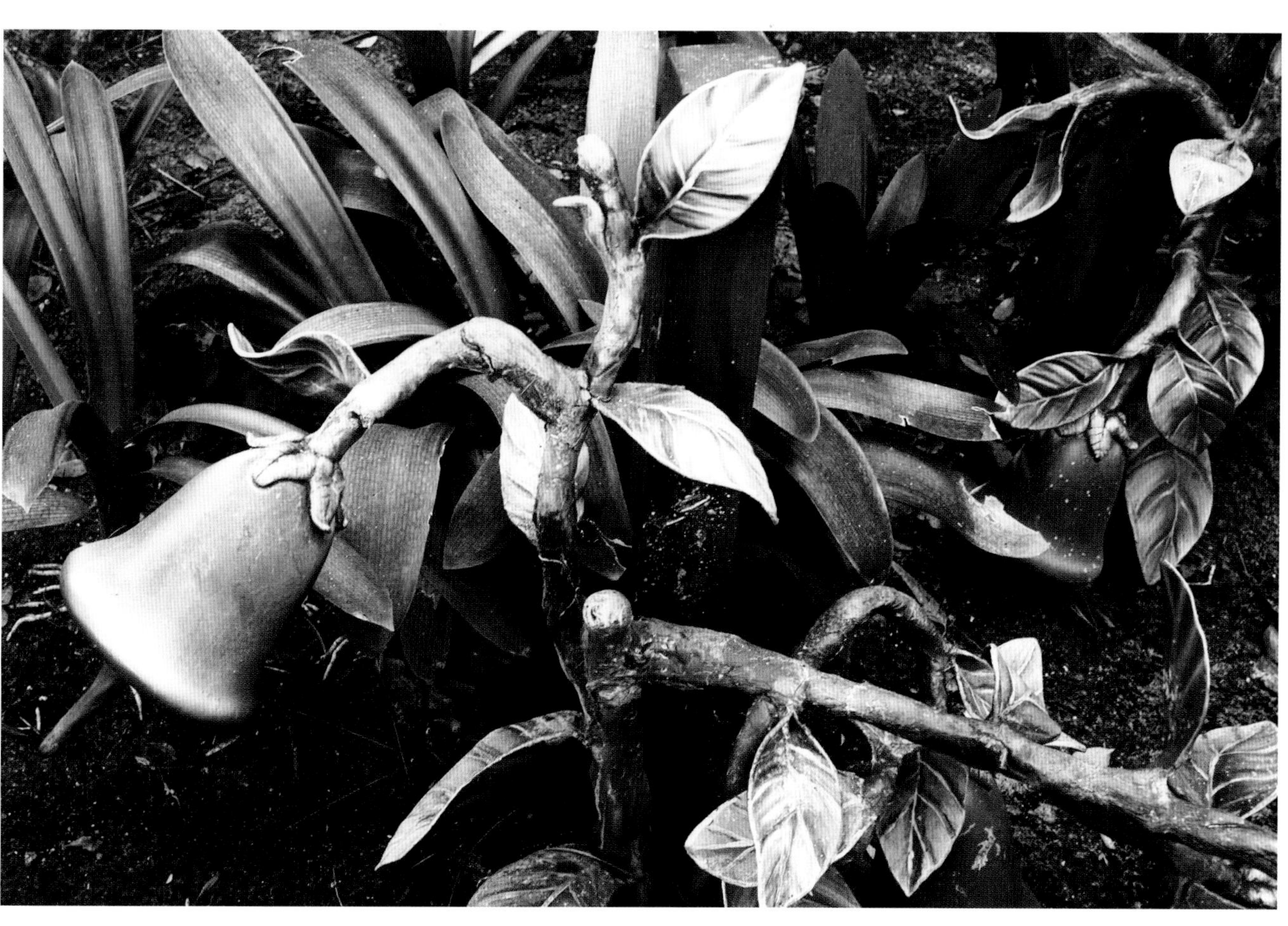

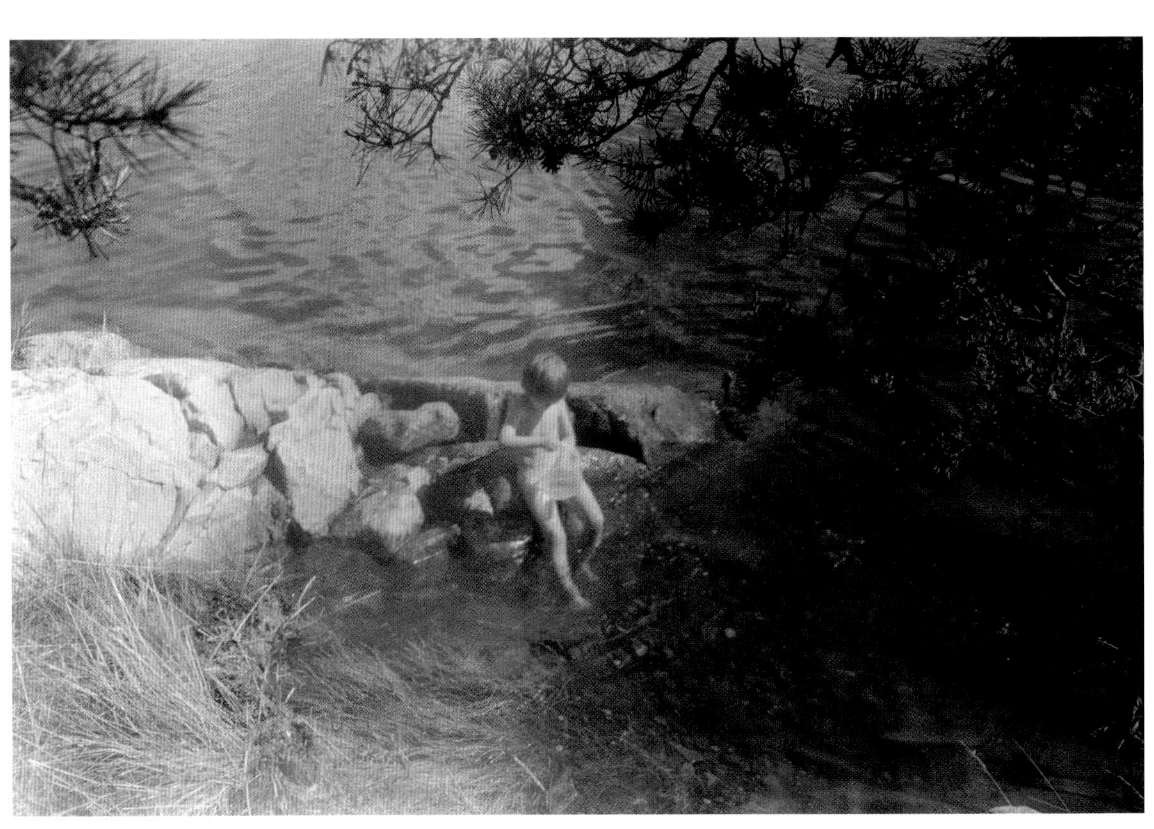

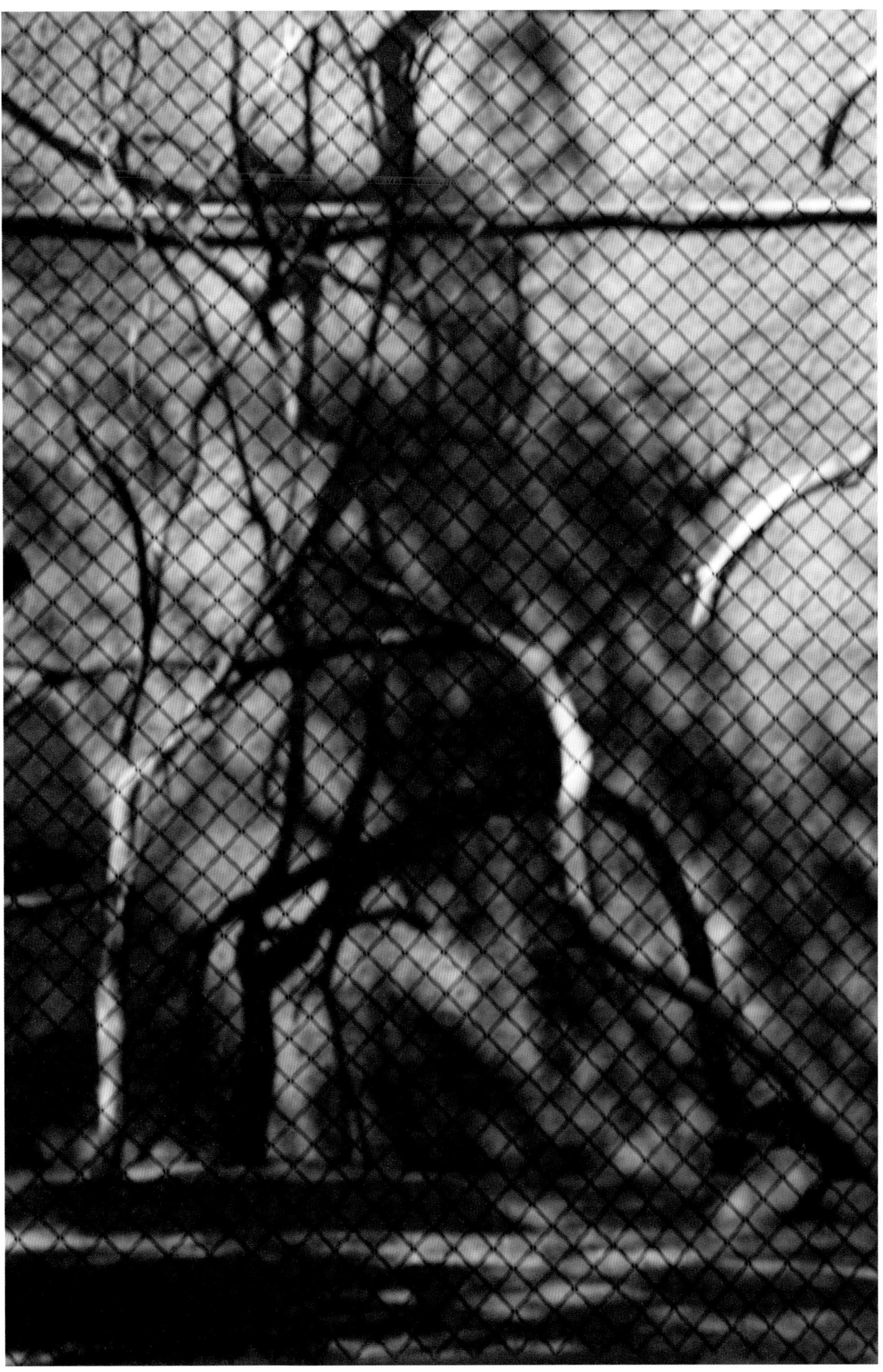

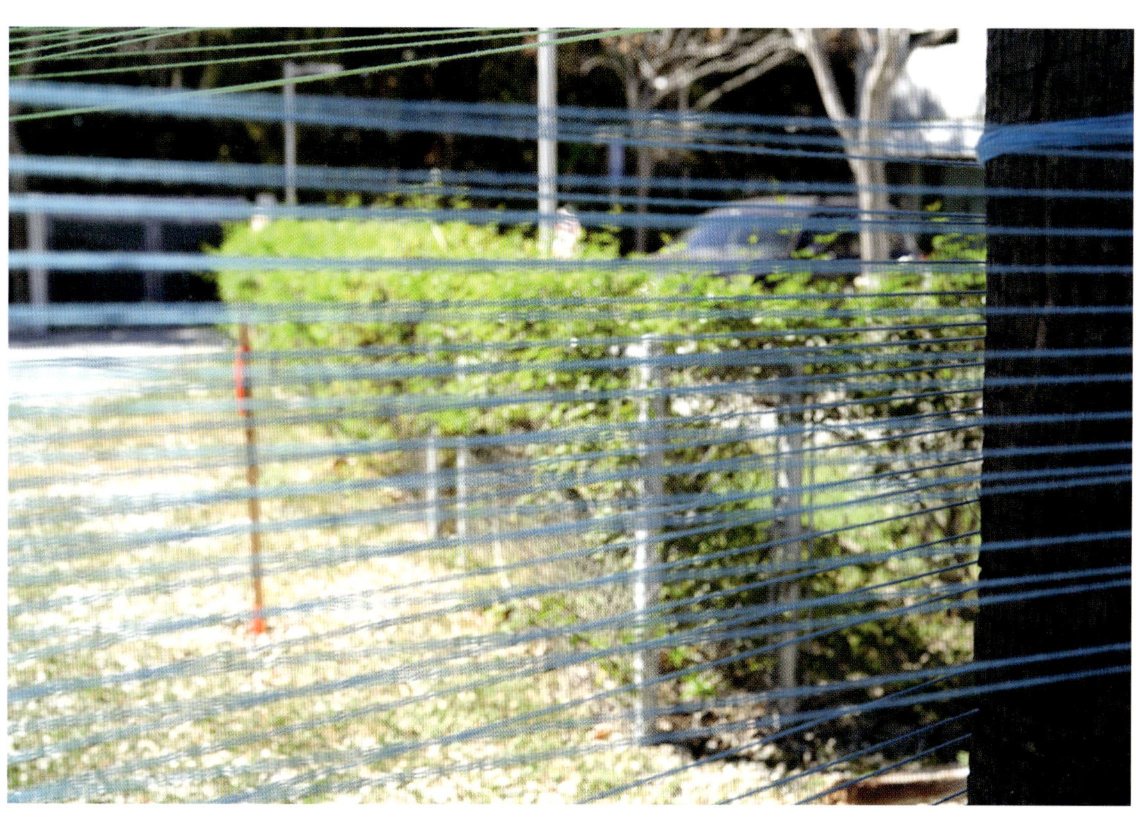

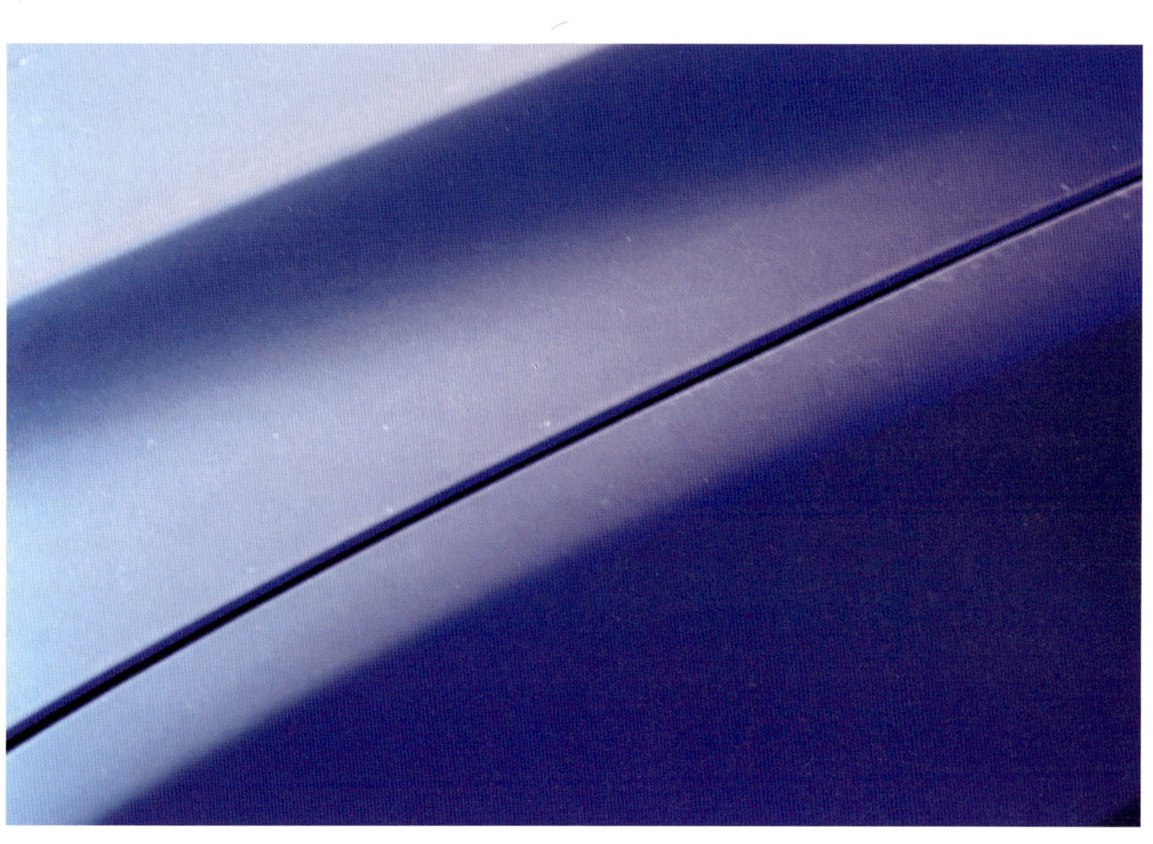

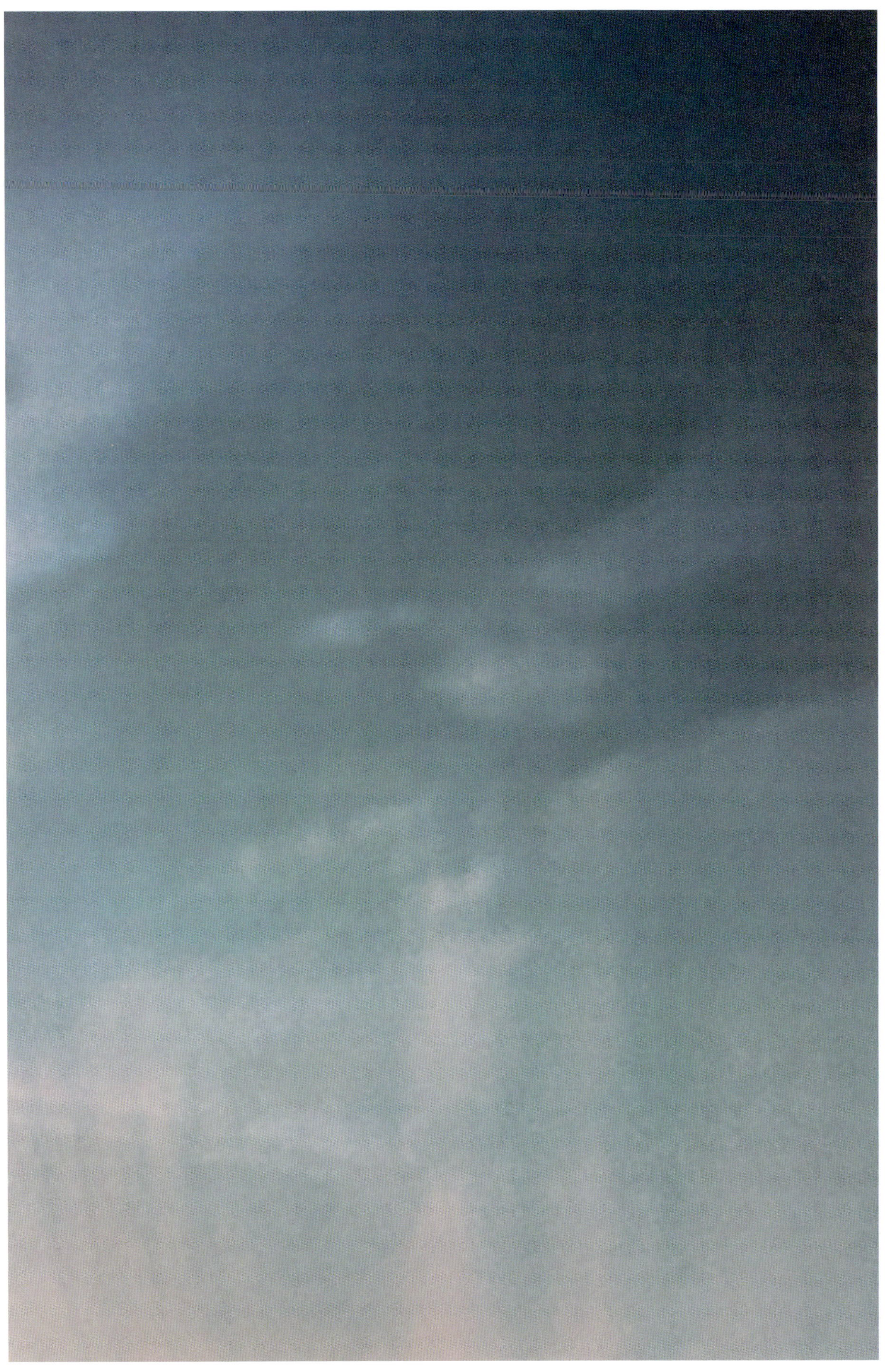

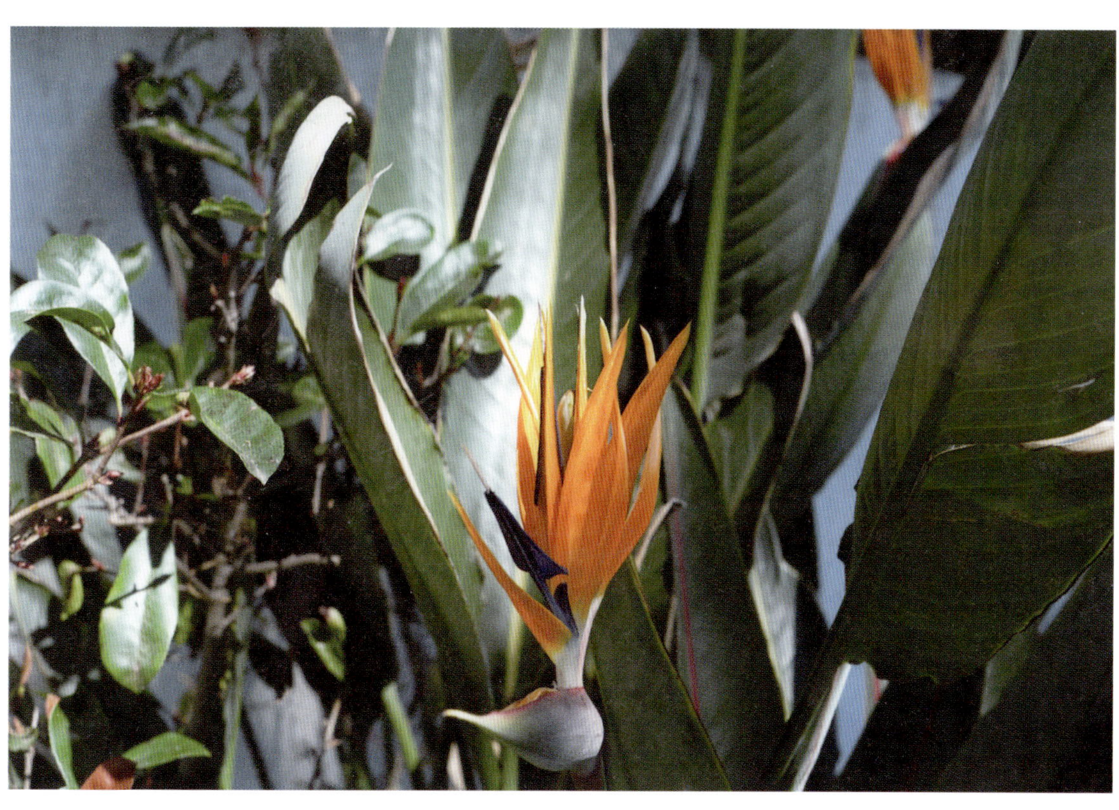

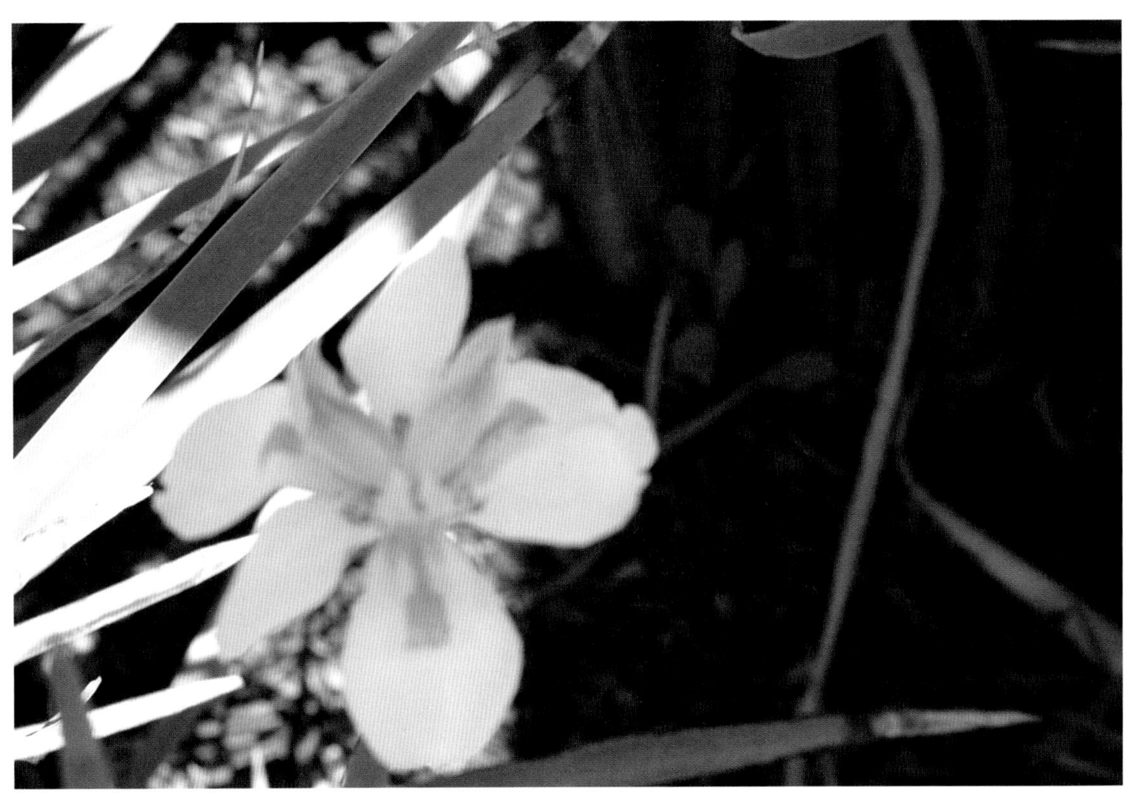

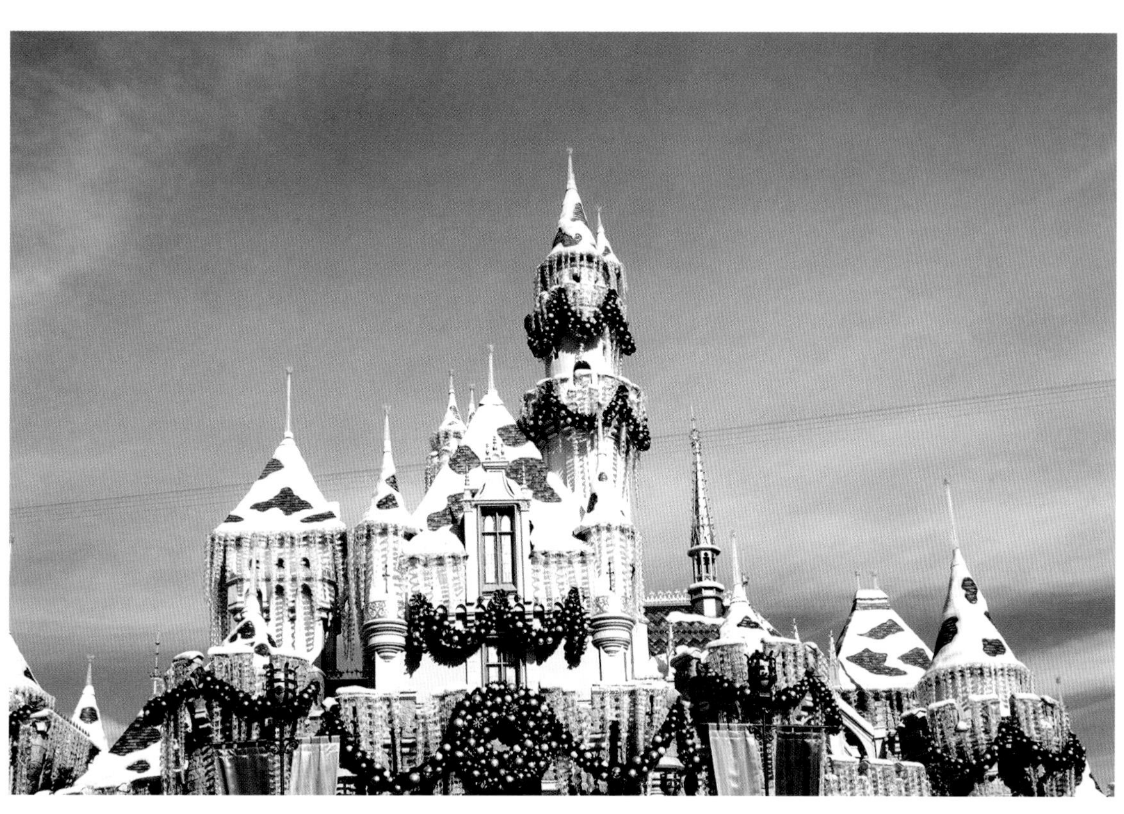

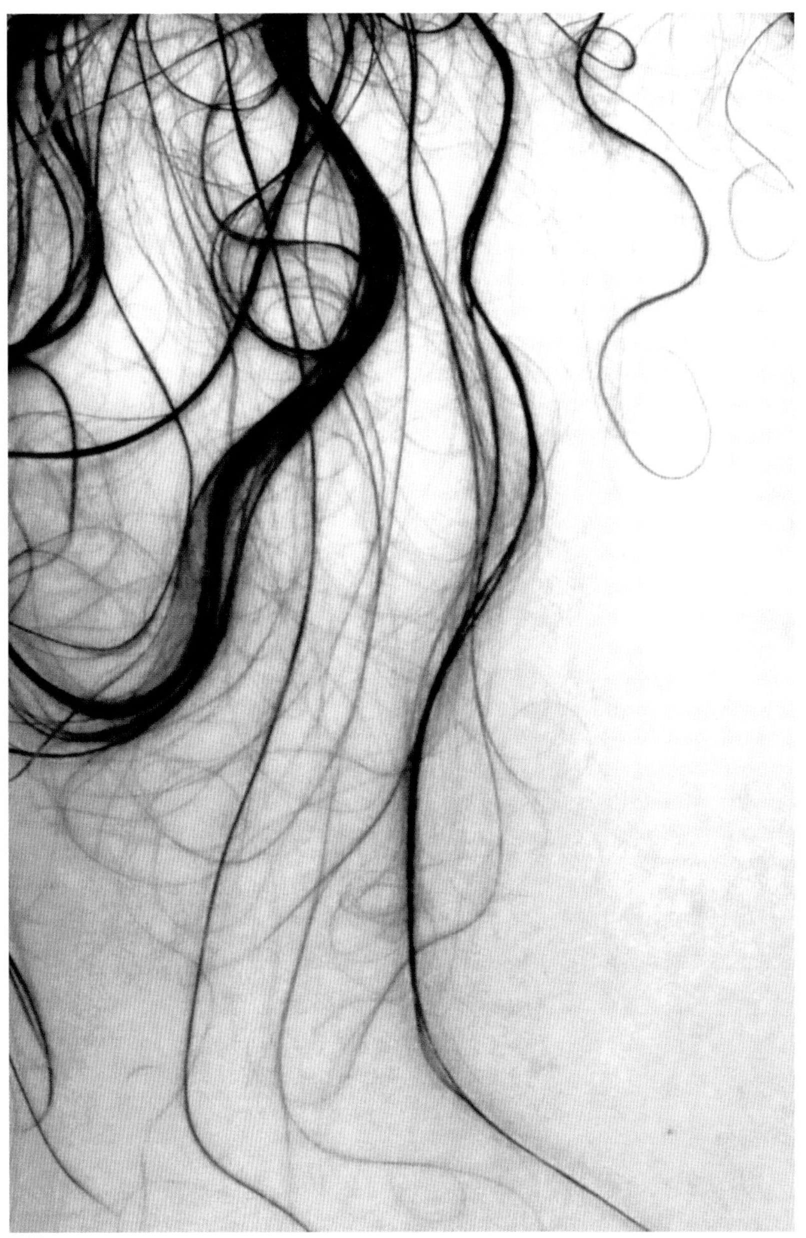

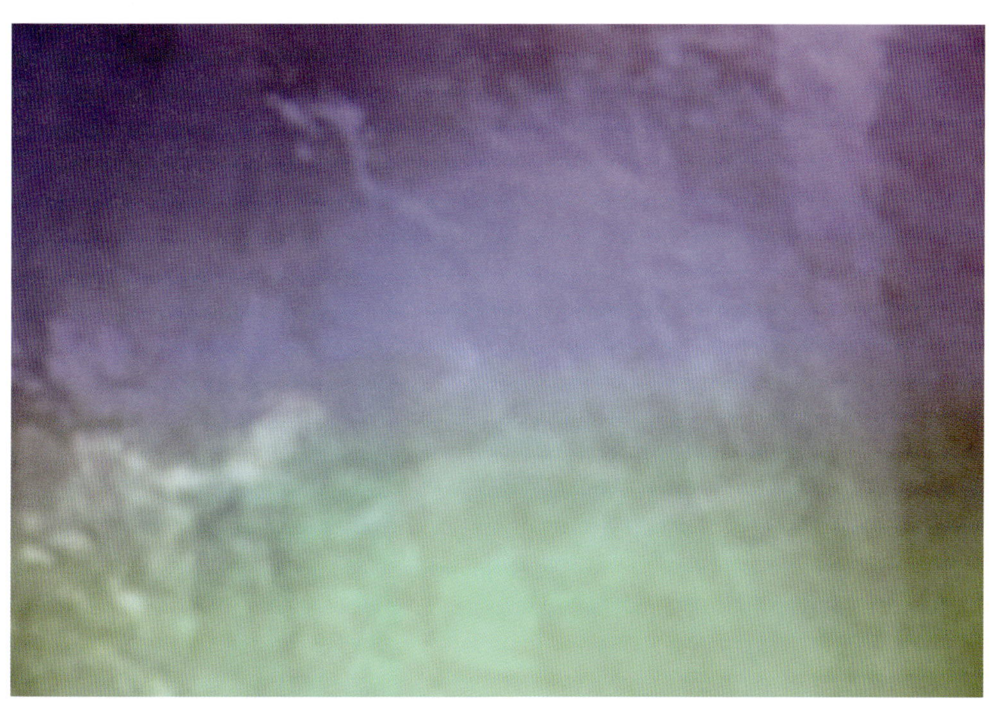

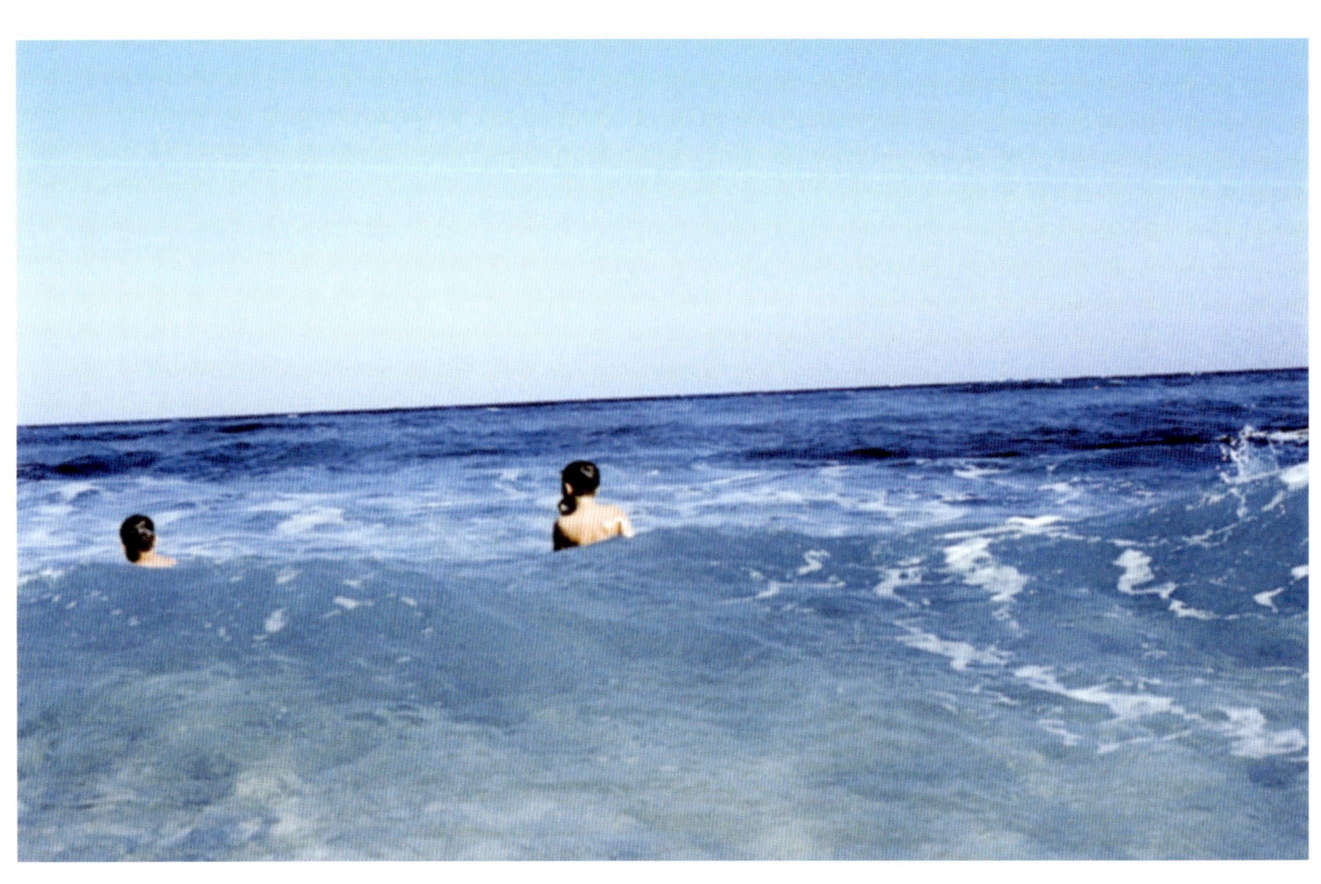

The Uncor

Sinziana

scious Eye

Ravini

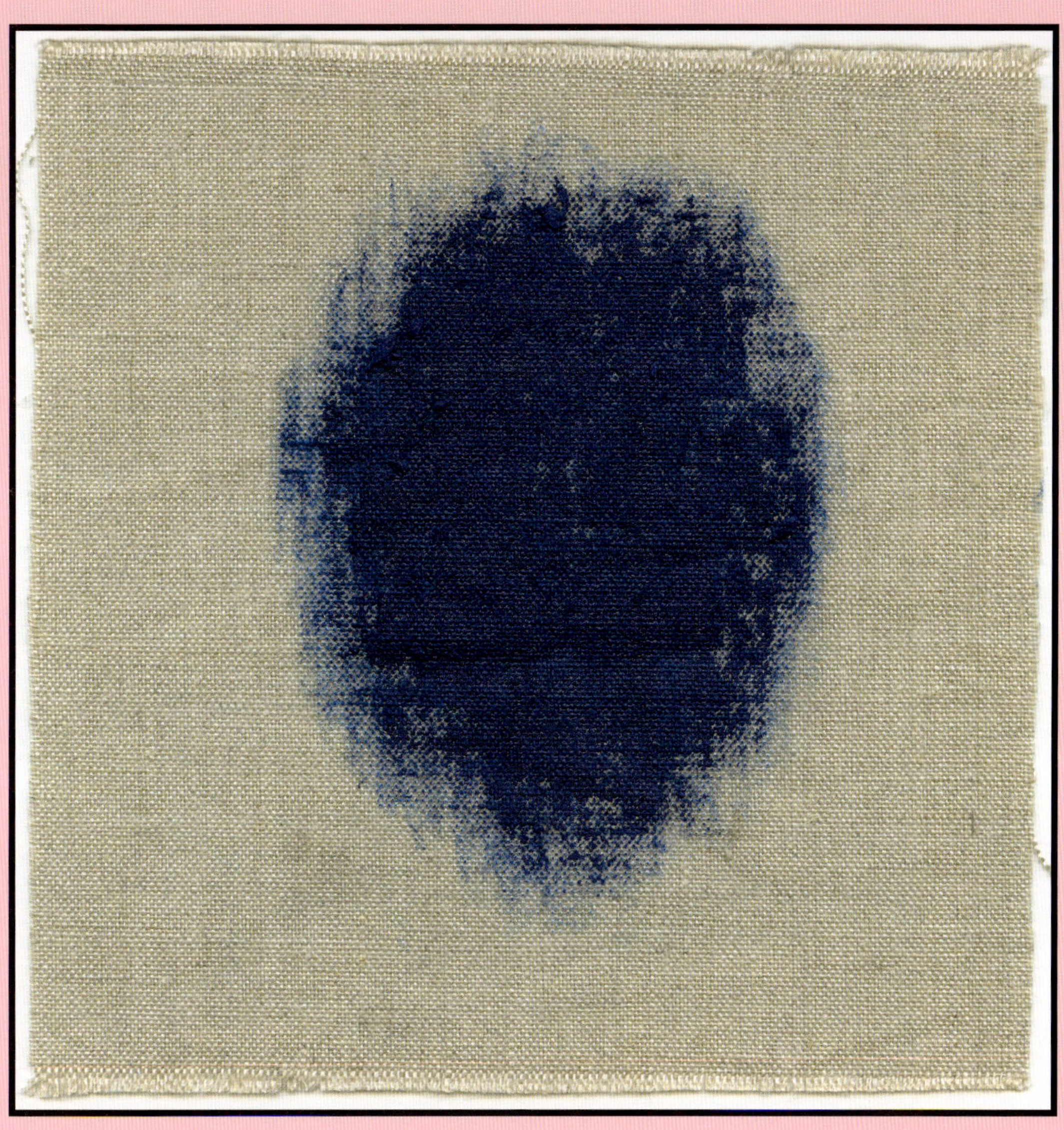

MAY 2024
?
X
eternity
AION
CHRONOS
Cosmic Rhythms
Messures Time
SUN
ZODIAC
Willing to STAY live
PRE PAUSE

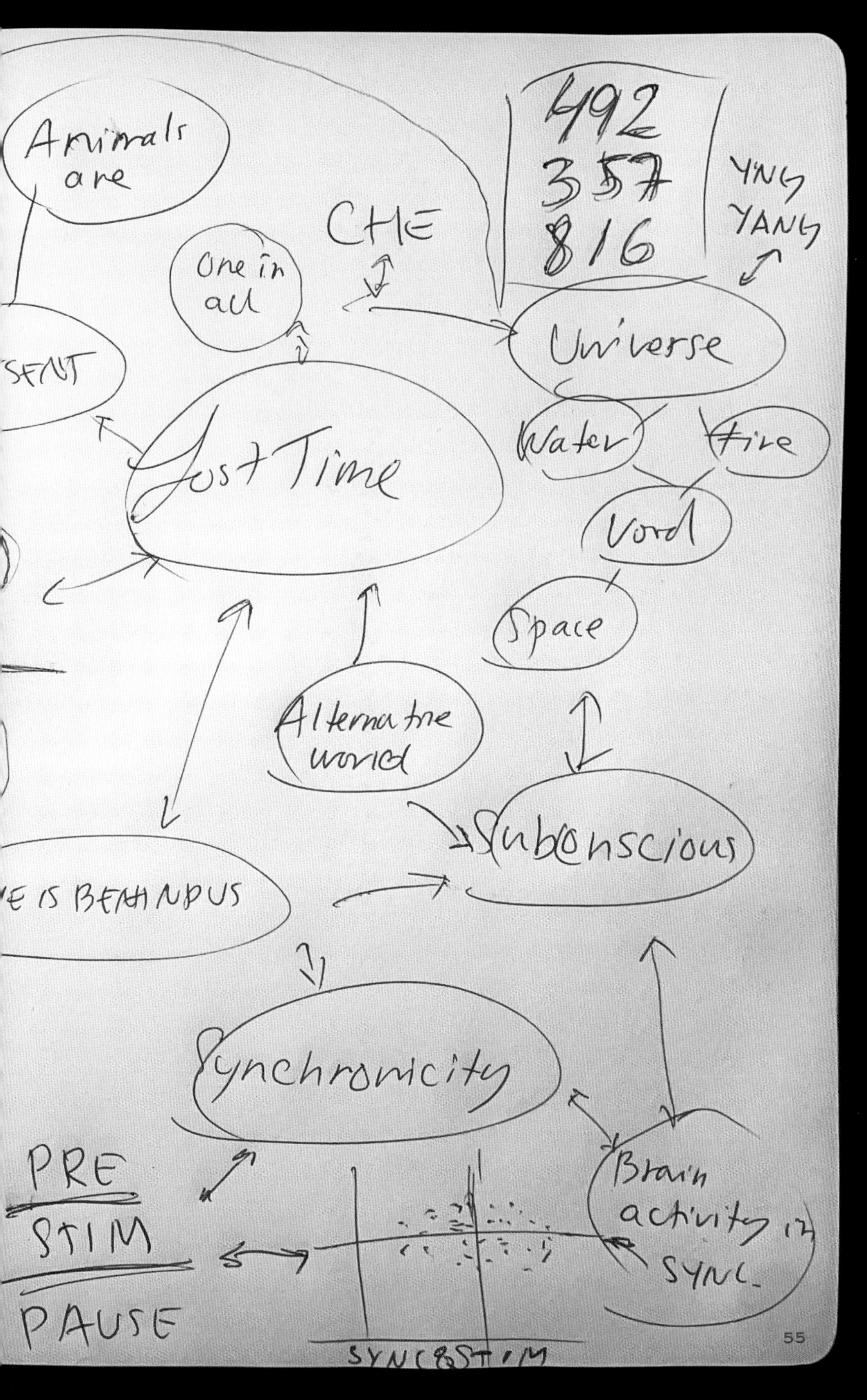

Animals are
One in all
CHE
492
357
816
YING YANG
Universe
PRESENT
Lost Time
Water
Fire
Vord
Space
Alternative world
IS BEHIND US
Subconscious
Synchronicity
PRE
STIM
PAUSE
Brain activity (?)
SYNC
SYNC & STIM
55

"Artmaking is making the invisible, visible," claimed Marcel Duchamp. This was not a metaphysical but a materialistic declaration, referring to the artist's power to elevate everyday objects to the status of art through the simple act of selection and presentation. Louise Enhörning follows Duchamp's dictum in two ways. First, by liberating objects from their usual contexts to frame and rearrange them unexpectedly, thus inviting the viewer to see them with fresh eyes and consider their symbolic significance. Second, by using groundbreaking camera technologies like the ELF method developed by researchers at Lund University in Sweden that captures light not visible to humans or animals. In both cases, the result is a delicate and sensual photography open to multiple readings, which aligns with another of Duchamp's beliefs: "the spectator makes the picture."

In Enhörning's work, we seldom know what we are looking at—in *Hole I* (2024), for example, what seems to be a crevice in a mountain takes on an ambiguity, referring to the negativity of the lack as well as the positivity of an opening to a new dimension. It's as if Enhörning were trying to photograph the unconscious, the "optical unconscious," a concept of Walter Benjamin's that Rosalind Krauss developed in her eponymous art-historical study from 1993. In her book, Krauss explains that the eye does not work like a camera: the brain filters out some information while adding visual elements to manipulate the real. If psychoanalysis discovers what the conscious mind cannot know, photography discovers the optical unconscious, a visual dynamic the eye cannot see.

Enhörning is mapping what can be both seen and not seen as she explores the ways in which memories are embedded within landscapes and objects. Her compositions, which often disrupt or isolate, stretch or compress, cut or dismantle different aspects of a single object, often blur the boundaries between past, present, and future, inviting viewers to engage with the cyclical nature of time and the moments that only a camera can catch. *Taken by Trees* (2023) shows a blurred young woman looking up in front of green foliage, and *Farfar och Pappa* (2004) presents a portrait by the artist's grandfather of himself and her father, creating a mise en abyme of memories. Enhörning often employs techniques such as long exposures, multiple exposures, and blurring effects to convey a sense of fluidity and spatial ambiguity, for example in work like *In Another Life* (2023), *Tomorrowland* (2023), *L'hiver* (2004), *Earth: Four Elements* (2024), and *Ways of Looking* (2024). It doesn't matter if we are in Tuscany or Stockholm, if it's winter or summer—time and space are deconstructed in favor of a melancholic gaze both mourning its lost object and discovering it anew. Sometimes the melancholia is twisted by a sense of humor, like in *Bag of Life* (2024), where we see a bag full of *livsmedel* (groceries in Swedish, literally "life means"), and sometimes it bursts out in an ecstatic celebration of life, like in *Ancient Swim* (2024), where we see a two boys swimming, *Aeneas* (2024), where we see a child immersing himself in water, or *Perfect Time* (2024), where we see a cherry tree in bloom.

Drawing inspiration from Marxist philosophy, Enhörning disrupts traditional hierarchies to question prevailing systems of value and exclusion, of what is admired or not, lost or forgotten, constantly giving personal myth a universal dimension. Her focus on details can sometimes verge on the fetishistic, like when she shows the carnality of a flower (*New Eros*, 2024) or the phallic contour of a car's surface (*Aphrodite's Flower*, 2024). When she distances herself from the studied subject, the image can become iconic—for example, the lonely woman holding a bag on a street in Paris, in *Valeska: First Years in Paris* (2006).

Enhörning's photographs serve as doors to alternative worlds, inviting viewers to enter realms where the familiar is rendered unfamiliar, the normal paranormal—for example, *Aphrodite's Terrasse* (2021), where the vivid sunlight gives the scenery a sacred dimension. Jungian psychology informs Enhörning's exploration of archetypal imagery and the depths of the collective unconscious. And this universal language seems to have deep affinities with the general and universal language of Google Images and symbols of humanity. Physics, including the study of daylight and electromagnetic radiation, also influences Enhörning. She manipulates visual elements by letting the power of light transform ordinary scenes into transcendent moments of revelation, like in *Lost Time* (2024), where the image looks like both a colorful test print and a portal into another dimension. We also encounter reflections on finitude and the fetishization of death, like the crown of skulls in *Kingdom of Bohemia: Church of Death* (1992), which at first glance looks like a crystal chandelier.

Animals, seasons, mountains, and seas feature prominently in Enhörning's visual narratives, symbolizing themes of renewal and the eternal rhythms of nature. Her seductive compositions evoke a deep reverence for the natural world, for the here and now, inviting viewers to contemplate both their place within the broader ecosystem and the impermanence of human experience. For what is photography if not a fixation of life and its inconsistency? Furthermore, Enhörning's photography reflects the wish to control the uncontrollable, the way children's games succeed in creating something out of nothing and try to master their surroundings through the creation of microworlds with their own rules that are hidden or incomprehensible to the grownup eye. It's as if her gaze never left childhood's imaginary playground.

Through her manipulation of the imaginary, the optical unconscious, and visual storytelling, Enhörning invites us to reconsider our perceptions of reality and embark on a transformative exploration of the human experience, where loss is transformed into gain and sadness into a celebration of the unbearable lightness of being. One can see her work as a testament to photography's power to illuminate the hidden dimensions of our inner and outer worlds and the interconnectedness of all things. It might sound grandiose, but it's not. It's simple, yet the simplest things are sometimes the hardest. As George Sand once wrote, "Simplicity is the most difficult thing to secure in this world; it is the last limit of experience and the last effort of genius."

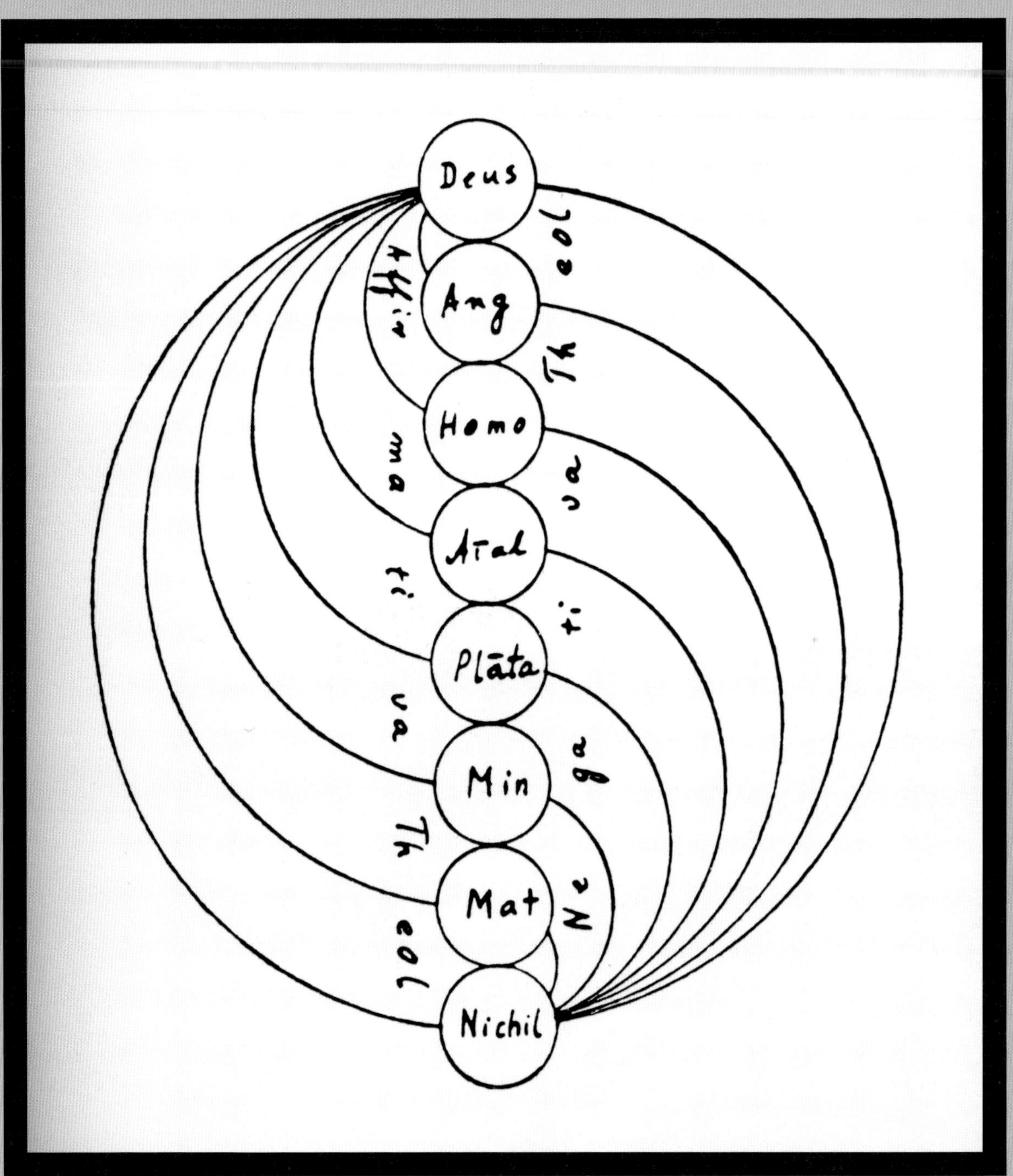

Deus
Ang
Homo
Atal
Plāta
Min
Mat
Nichil
Affir
Theol
Th
ma
va
ti
ti
ua
ga
Th
Ne
eol

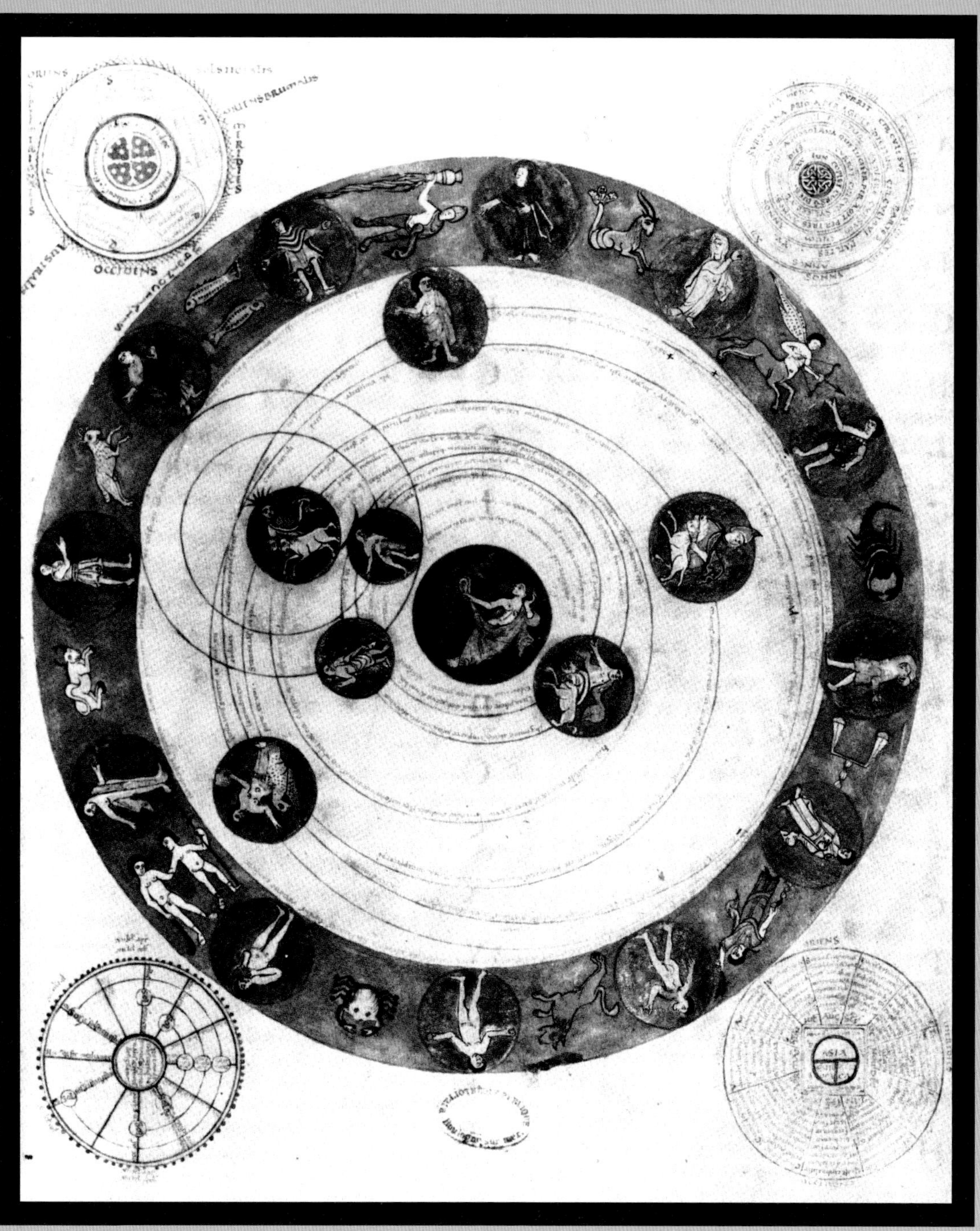

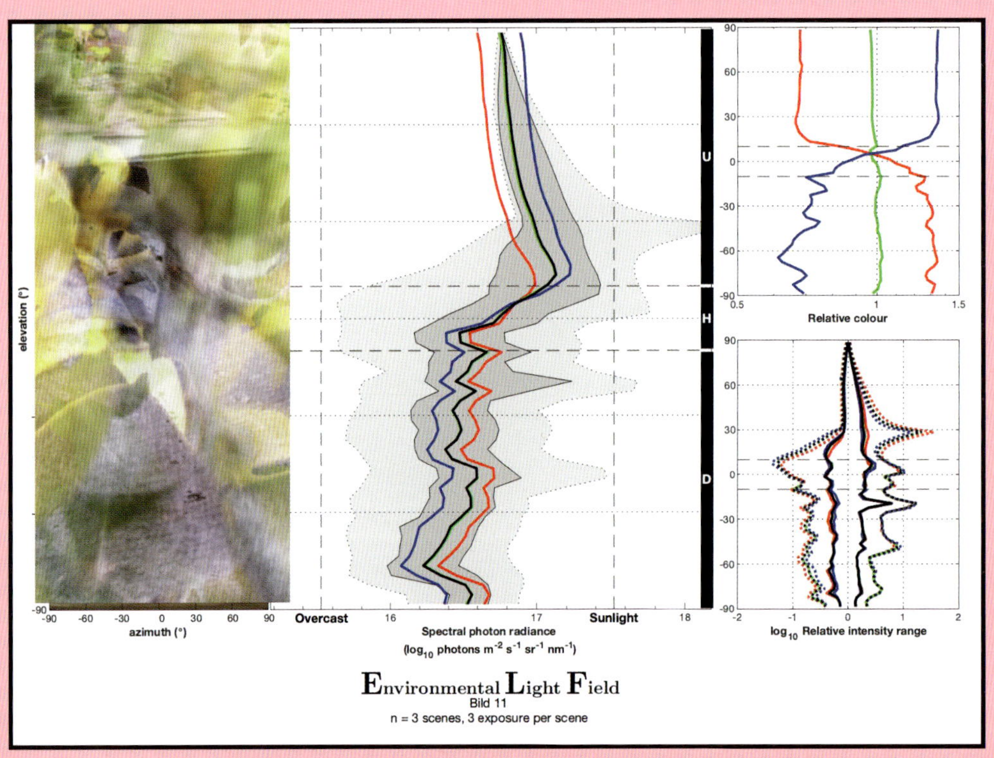

Environmental Light Field

Bild 11

n = 3 scenes, 3 exposure per scene

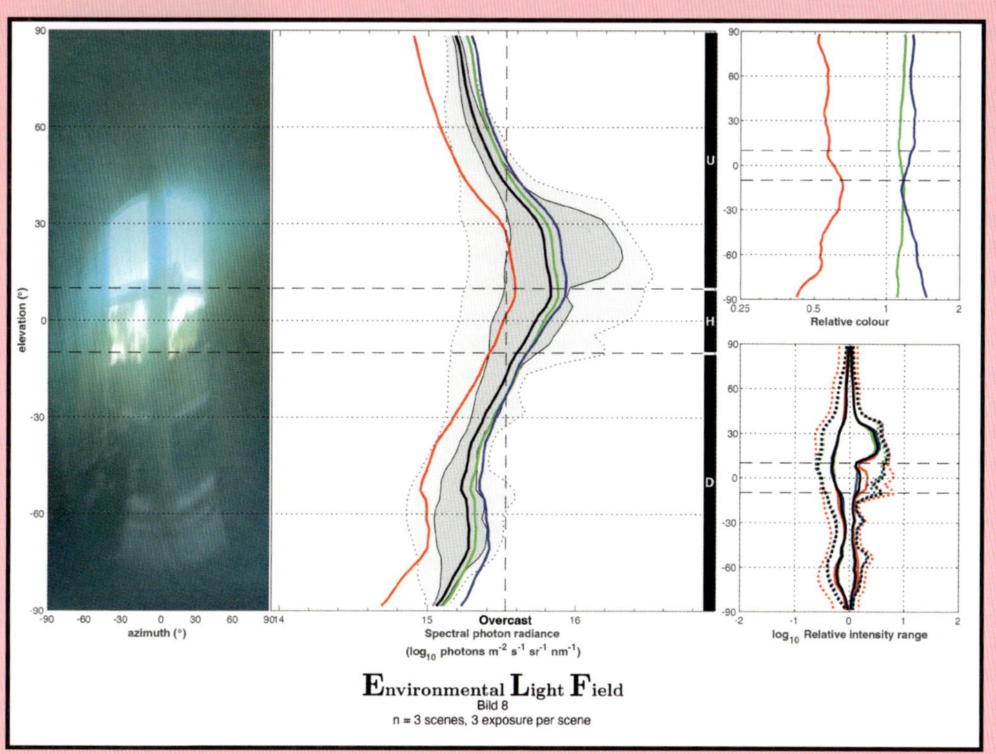

Environmental **L**ight **F**ield
Bild 8
n = 3 scenes, 3 exposure per scene

LIST of WORKS

p. 45
Circular Time, 2015
Giclée print from digital photograph,
dimensions variable
Home, 7 rue Saint-Claude, Paris

p. 47
Synchronicity, 2024
Giclée print from digital photograph,
dimensions variable
Stockholm

pp. 48–49
Aphrodite's Terrasse, 2021
C-print from 35mm film negative,
dimensions variable
Aphrodite Beach, Cyprus

p. 50
Hole I, 2024
C-print from 35mm film negative,
dimensions variable
Stone formation, Uvön, Sweden, 2016

p. 51
The Sensibility of the Rain, 2024
Giclée print from digital photograph,
dimensions variable
Location unknown, 2020

pp. 52–53
Heron City: Map of the Summer, 2021
Water sculpture with 60 cyanotypes,
257 × 193 cm
Installation view,
Östermalmstorg subway station, Stockholm

p. 54
Bag of Life, 2024
C-print from 35mm film negative,
dimensions variable
Summer fruit in a bag,
Slussen, Stockholm, 2023

p. 55
Aeneas, 2024
C-print from 35mm film negative,
dimensions variable
Otto, Marrakech, 2023

p. 57
Valeska: First Years in Paris, 2006
C-print from 35mm film negative,
dimensions variable
Valeska, passage Saint-Sébastien, Paris

p. 58
Lost Time, 2024
Giclée print from digital photograph,
24 x 30 cm
Light spectrum, Marrakech, 2023

p. 59
Transformation, 2024
Giclée print from digital photograph,
dimensions variable
Carsten's bird, 2021

p. 60
Perception of a Mountain, 2024
Giclée print from digital photograph,
dimensions variable
Los Angeles Zoo, 2022

p. 61
Yellow Garden, 2021
ELF image, 40 × 40 cm
Easter, Skåne, Sweden

p. 62
Aphrodite Beach II, 2021
C-print from 35mm film negative,
dimensions variable
Aphrodite Beach, Cyprus

pp. 94
Ancient Swim, 2024
C-print from 35mm film negative,
dimensions variable
Otto and another kid swimming,
Cyprus, 2021

p. 98
Linear Time, 2024
Giclée print from digital photograph,
dimensions variable
Stockholm

p. 99
Blue Hole, 2024
Oil pastel on linen, 14 × 12 cm

pp. 100–101
Mindmap Lost Time, 2024
Pen, notebook

p. 106
"Spheres of Existence"
From Carolus Bovillus, *De nihilo,* 1510

p. 107
Zodiac, ninth century
Handmade, France

p. 108
ELF data for *Yellow Garden,* 2021

p. 109
ELF data for *Green Window,* 2021

In February 2021, Louise Enhörning collaborated with the Lund Vision Group in the Department of Biology at Lund University, utilizing a new method to read light. This innovative camera technology reveals light that is invisible to both humans and animals. The resulting images uncover new realities through the ELF (environmental light field) method developed at the university.

Louise Enhörning
Lost Time, Aphrodite Beach

With an essay by	Sinziana Ravini
Graphic Design	Martin Falck
Editor	Max Bach
Printer	ManMade, Tallinn
Paper	Inlay: Arctic Volume White 150g
	Cover: Arctic Volume White 250g

Thank you: Anna Ahonen, Prof. Dan-E Nilsson, Elin Unnes, Hannes Hetta, Helena Danielsson, Ilaria Bombelli, Mamma, Marie Birde, Martin Falck, Max Bach, Mousse Publishing, Nina Tahko, Otto, Pappa, Sinziana Ravini, Stefan Fält, Valeska, and Victoria Bergsman

Published and distributed by

Mousse Publishing
Contrappunto s.r. l.
Via Pier Candido Decembrio 28
20137, Milan–Italy
moussemagazine.it

First edition: 2024
Printed in Estonia
ISBN 978-88-6749-636-5
€ 30 / $ 35